NEW ECONOMIC ORDER
The Global Economic Matrix (GEM)

*In our world today,
no other issue is as deeply rooted
in our activities and state of well-being.*

It is the critical key 'to change all things'.

It is the monetary system itself.

And all things are interconnected.

*As represented by the
Flower of Life / Sacred Geometry
illustration used on the cover.*

NEW ECONOMIC ORDER
The Global Economic Matrix (GEM)

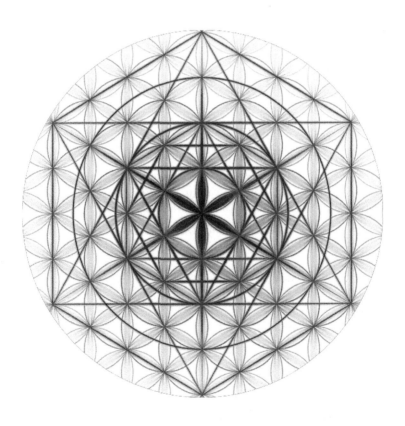

Richard E. Kotlarz

Other articles and writings
by Richard Kotlarz
available at: richardkotlarz.com

Email: richkotlarz@gmail.com

Book design & editing: Elaine Kain
using LibreOffice open-source software

Published by Tales & Testaments: An Imprint of
The Center for American Studies at Concord

ISBN-13: 978-0-9642968-4-8

"Usury's Curse"

Hark the entreaties of the broken
Souls who have borne usury's curse,
Debt-money's train of death and woes.
The huddled betimes scarce awoken
Soon to find wit and will aburst,
The hour, impending, no man knows.

The meek get ready to inherit the earth,
The earth prepares to receive the sky,
The youth anon will discover a future,
So We declare it -
and now you know "Why".

\- Richard

Endorsement

Why read another book, friends? Who has time (eternity aside) — to read particularly a book about *economics*, the *"dismal science"* itself? God* forbid/bid… help us!

These questions are, perhaps, best answered by those "in the know," the two gentlemen quoted below. If their words speak to you, I invite you to read this book and discover the 'gems' within. It is indeed both a pleasure and honor to endorse this work for brother Richard.

Dedicated to the fulfillment of the "promise" of We the People -

Stuart-Sinclair Weeks,
Founder, The Center for American Studies: www.concord-ium.us
Fellow Inaugurator, The Bretton Woods Monetary Institute & Festival: https://brettonwoods.us

* *"In God We Trust"*…. Inscribed on our very currency.

"All the perplexities, confusion, and distress in America arise, not from defects of the Constitution or Confederation; not from any want of honor or virtue, as much as downright ignorance of the nature of coin, credit, and circulation." - John Adams

"The modern banking system manufactures money out of nothing. The process is perhaps the most astounding piece of sleight of hand that was ever invented. Banking was conceived in iniquity and born in sin. Bankers own the Earth. Take it away from them, but leave them the power to **create** *money, and with the flick of the pen they will* **create** *enough money to buy it back again. However, take this great power* [to **create** money out of nothing] *away from bankers and all great fortunes like mine will disappear, and they ought to disappear. For then this would be a better and happier world to live in.* ***But, if you want to continue to be slaves of the banks and pay the cost of your own slavery, then let bankers continue to create money and control credit.****"* [**emphasis** added] - Sir Josiah Stamp, former Director of the Bank of England, at the time the second richest man in the British empire. *Acres USA Magazine, "The Owners", April 1991.*

Foreword

My journey with Richard started...

...when I asked him a seemingly simple question: *What is Money?* I sensed there was something inherently wrong within our financial system, yet I could not identify its true nature or cause. The concepts Richard shared answered this question at a depth that few economic scholars achieve. His years of studying this topic to get to 'the heart of the matter' developed into a greater understanding that is missing in our current state of financial affairs.

Richard's 'monetary exploration' reminds me of *Plato's Cave*, wherein one person breaks free of his shackles and discovers the light. It is a painful path of both self-discovery and redefining one's world views, letting go of the socially-acceptable 'shadow world' and attempting to bring others out of the cave. I find the 'expert chatter' on monetary matters today similar to the cave-dwellers' debate on 'what is the shadow and what is it saying?' As in the cave, few people want to endure the pain of learning 'what they thought they knew all along was wrong' - and they will rush in panic back to the familiar comfort of the world they know, even if it is a dark, dreary and stressful existence.

'Money' is not easily defined, and the perception of 'what it is' has as many fuzzy responses as defining something by the shadow on the wall and muted sounds echoing around us. We must move beyond this discussion and achieve a clarity of vision if we are to understand 'it' and the interactions in our lives.

I asked a mutual friend once what would we have if 'money' disappeared overnight. With a stricken look, Wayne replied, "There would be riots and people starving, destruction and chaos, collapse of society..."

I replied, "We'd have exactly the same things we had the day before; the same resources, labor, buildings, energy, skills and talents. But we wouldn't have bits of paper or numbers to trade, and we wouldn't know how to function. Yet we consider ourselves to be of superior intelligence!"

I cannot easily explain this uniquely human conundrum, yet Richard 'makes sense out of it'. His cumulative studies developed into this book. Anyone who reads it and absorbs the insights presented will find their perceptions shifted, as the shadows and myths of 'money' are dispersed with revelations of clarity and recognition of its true nature. In our world today, no other issue is as deeply rooted in our activities and state of well-being. It is the critical key 'to change all things'.

I have learned much by assisting Richard with his articles and manuscripts; indeed, I owe him a debt of gratitude. These are a few of the 'gems' hidden in this book, in Richard's own words:

...To be sure, there were many cries for increased regulation, but "regulation" will not fix the basic flaw at the heart of the monetary system... (page 31)

...The individual and cultural denial on this wise has given rise to all manner of abstract theories... As the arguments grow more vociferous or nuanced, these simple factors are multiplied and played against each other in ever-greater displays of financial sophistication. The result is essentially a churning of the intellectual waters whereby the transparency of the economic order is totally obscured. This can be remedied by returning to common sense... (page 44)

...The monetary franchise is legally, structurally and morally out of place now. I see no problem in principle with restoring it as the political arm of the social order, which is what it should properly be. (page 74)

...We should first discover why the UN is apparently so dysfunctional in its current configuration. The root of the answer I believe is that it is laboring under an impossible condition. That is, it is the representative body of a world of nations which cannot complete their own domestic market cycles. (page 99)

Once we 'know' what money is, the next question is: What are going to do about it? ...

The journey continues... Elaine Kain

NEW ECONOMIC ORDER
The Global Economic Matrix (GEM)

- CONTENTS -

- THE GLOBAL ECONOMIC MATRIX -

CHAPTER 1
THE PRESENT SYSTEM

The "Debt"-Based Nature of the Dollar:

Virtually every dollar in circulation has come into existence as the principal amount of a "loan" from a private bank. The money the banker disperses does not come out of funds on deposit in his vault, but rather he creates the money with the "writing of the check". The borrower takes the check, and then goes out and spends the proceeds for whatever purpose he took out the loan to satisfy. By the terms of the contract, the banker will demand to be paid back over a prescribed time period, not only the principal amount of the loan, but also a compounding "interest" charge. It should be noted that a quantity of dollars equivalent to the principal amount were issued and spent into circulation, and so these are available in the money supply. The dollars required to pay the "interest", however, were never issued. The critical question, then, that underlies the current monetary system is, "Where will the money to make the interest payments on bank loans come from?"

It should be noted further that virtually every dollar in circulation was created and issued via "loans" from commercial banks. The borrower can be any individual or corporate entity (individual consumers, entrepreneurs, corporations, state and local governments), and even the Federal Government. In the private sector the form of such "loans" run the gamut from house mortgages, car payments and student loans to payday lending and revolving lines of credit. It is not commonly realized that when a consumer swipes a credit card for a retail purchase, the total that pops up on the register is newly created money that did not exist the moment before the swipe. It represents the proceeds from a "loan" that the card holder has just contracted with a bank (*which is why every credit card has the name of a bank on it*).

The aggregate of the principal proceeds from all bank loans being borrowed and spent into circulation constitutes the money supply. The period of time between the borrowing and the payback is what gives money duration so that it is available to circulate. This is the process by which the monetary pool is formed and maintained. Theoretically, the amount of money in circulation should be sufficient to pay back all those "loans", but there is a hitch, and the problems it spawns are legion. While the money necessary to pay back the principal amount of such "loans" is by the nature of the process made available, the credits required to "pay back" the "interest" are not. The upshot is that the participants in the economy cannot on the whole pay their "debts" (principal plus "interest"), while still maintaining an adequate money supply.

But, one could say, loans are taken out and paid back all the time. Where, then, is this "interest" money coming from? The answer is that as people make "interest" payments on loans that come due, the money to do so is being subtracted from the principal proceeds of loans still in circulation. This creates a particular problem, which is that when the time comes for people to make payments on these later loans, the money supply will have experienced a net shortfall of funds available to pay back their principal amounts equal to the amount that was subtracted to make earlier "interest" payments, plus the holders of this latter "debt" will have to search about to find the money to "pay back" their "interest" as well.

If one does a bit of math (and it's not much math) is evident that there is only one way that this situation can be managed. That is, participants in the economy are effectively forced to borrow more money into circulation on a continuous basis so that the interest payments on old debt can be cash-flowed, and a money supply sufficient for the needs of commerce maintained in circulation. What is more, this debt rotation must not only be kept up, but increased on an exponential basis to accommodate the compounding growth of "interest due" inculcated in these debt-money contracts. The economy as a whole, then, becomes caught up in an increasing "debt" spiral that it has no practical way of escaping as long as this private-bank-loan transaction remains the mode by which money is created. This then becomes the engine of mammon that drives, directly or indirectly, virtually all money-related problems in the world today. This is true whether they are nominally economic or not. Money isn't everything, but in our modern global world it must be taken into account to do anything.

To be sure, this plays out in extremely complex ways, but the source of the seemingly unresolvable monetary churning that has overcome the economy at all levels can always be traced back to the sleight of mind inculcated in the initial private-bank-loan transaction. Outwardly speaking, the entire range of financial anomalies extant in the world today arise from this one simple cause. The key to navigating the intricacies of the current financial chaos, from local to global, is to not lose sight of this singular fact.

How the Monetary Problem Unfolds:

Let us track in greater detail what happens when a payment is made on a private bank loan. The funds remitted to the bank are divided into two parts. One portion is applied to reducing the outstanding principal balance (amount of money still owed) on the loan, and the other is credited towards the paying the "interest". The money that is applied to the principal goes back out of circulation, and is extinguished on the banker's books in a reversal of the process by which it was created. It no longer exists.

The funds that are applied to the "interest", however, are credited to the account of an "investor". In this case "investor" is a euphemism for a creditor who is holding, directly or indirectly, the "debt"-contract written against the loan. Since this money is technically still in circulation, the "investor" could indeed spend it, but people who "invest" in such things generally don't do so with the grocery money. They are folks who are wealthy enough to have funds that they don't immediately need (or need at all, with respect to personal maintenance), or they are trustees of other peoples money who have been charged with the responsibility to "invest" it for maximum financial return (i.e. money earning money). They are therefore free and/or pledged to use the proceeds from these "interest" payments to buy still more bonds, stocks and mortgage contracts in the financial marketplace. As the "interest" payments on their "debt"-based-paper portfolios roll in, the money is "re-invested" into more "debt"-based paper. The net effect of this process is to transfer huge sums from the circulating monetary pool (where it was borrowed into circulation by people who need it to live on or do productive work), and into the hands of wealthy speculators or financial managers who, through the simple holding of debt contracts, are bidding to increase their wealth without the expenditure of productive effort.

This process results in a hoarding of money whose effect is twofold. Firstly, it effectively causes the available monetary pool to shrink, thereby depriving participants in the economy in the aggregate of the funds necessary to satisfy the loan contracts by which it was borrowed into circulation. Secondly, the resulting downward spiral of available money deprives the people in the economy of the ability to buy back the total output of what they produced.

Producers, Consumers and the Market Cycle:

There are fundamentally two types of players in the market cycle; i.e. producers and consumers. Within a sound producer/consumer rotation, the costs of the producer are all accounted for in the form of wages and profits. All the complexities and deceptive appearances notwithstanding, it really is that simple. We pay people for their work; we don't write checks to the earth for its resources. When people pick up their paychecks and profits from the productive sector, they go home and become consumers. Ideally the amount of money in their collective pockets should equal the cost to producers of bringing the available products to market. Value of goods and services produced will match the money available to buy them, exactly. Prices will tend to find their own equilibrium (like water finding its own level) in the collective haggling between the producing and consuming sectors, and the market will be cleared of whatever is produced.

When an "interest" charge is attached to the issuance of money, however, this equilibrium is subverted. Things have to be produced before they are consumed. When the worker takes his paycheck, or the businessman his profit, home, the first thing he does typically is to pay his bills. A portion of his remittances will go to pay down the principal amount of the loan, which represents the actual purchasing credits borrowed for past consumption. There will also be a portion that goes for "interest". This "interest" charge, however, is money that he does not receive anything tangible for, and constitutes therefore a net subtraction of purchasing power from what is available to the consumer to buy back the products of production. After paying his bills the consumer will put the remainder of his wage and/or profit into his pocket where it becomes spending money for groceries, gasoline, entertainment, or whatever else. The net result of this "interest" payment having been subtracted from his income stream is that the consuming sector will, in the aggregate, not be able to "afford" what it has itself produced. There is no possible manipulation of prices that will remedy this shortfall.

So, the question becomes – "What happens to the money remitted to the bank in these "interest" payments?" The answer is that it is retained as "earnings" by the "investors" who "own" the "debt instruments" that "back" these "loans". Such "owners" and "investors" could include stockholders in the bank, but more often are holders of private investment portfolios. These "earnings" could be spent into the market cycle also, thereby filling in their part of the money needed to clear the marketplace of goods and services produced, but since generally this is money excess to the investor's personal needs, it can be withheld from circulation until he finds the opportunity to "re-invest" it (i.e. "loan" it to someone). He is in effect holding these funds back from the general circulation until someone is willing to pay him to release them (at "interest", of course) back into the circulating stream. It is certain that someone will in fact feel obliged to ask for such a loan, for a twofold reason: (1) the money has to come back into circulation if the productive sector is to sell the remainder of its product, and (2) it will be needed by the consumer to make up for his shortfall in buying power.

If people were to quit borrowing, the "investor" would be forced to spend his proceeds back into the monetary stream, effectively foregoing the chance to profit further by charging "interest" on a loan. Theoretically, if this process went on long enough, the loans could be cleared without default on any contract, and all the money borrowed into circulation could go back to the bank. What makes this scenario for all practical purposes impossible is that it would extinguish the money supply. People need money with which to purchase the things they need almost every day, and so the possibilities for this winding down process to proceed very far are extremely limited, save at great human cost. We have need of a circulating medium, but by the nature of how the system is set up, we are effectively locked in a casino and forced to use its chips (Federal Reserve Notes) under "house rules" (i.e. rules imposed by the banking system).

To be sure, none of this is done consciously. For the most part people are merely trying earn a living, pay their debts, and carry out their fiduciary responsibilities (bankers and investors included). Furthermore, since everyone's "loan" money becomes quickly blended with everyone else's when it is spent into circulation, the money that is being subtracted from the monetary pool to pay the "interest" on a given loan is not identified with any other specific loan. It must be understood that what we are dealing with here are aggregate effects.

The upshot of the whole process is that the availability of funds in the money supply is constantly falling short of what is needed for the populace to pay its bills and carry on commerce. It attempts to survive for a time by continually expanding into new areas of "economic growth" in search of an expanding collateral basis for borrowing more money from banks, but this is a dog-chasing-its-tail-faster-and-faster game that can only go so far before it collapses in exhaustion. The cumulative "debt" compounds on an exponential basis, but physical and human enterprise that is trying to expand to match it cannot forever keep up.

The Hydraulic Loop Analogy:
To illustrate, the workings of a properly structured market cycle are analogous to a hydraulic loop. We can liken the productive factor in the economy to the pump, and the needs of the consumer to the end usage where its energy is expended. If there are no leaks in a hydraulic system, then every drop of fluid medium that leaves the pump will show up at the device which it drives, and in turn find its way back to the pump. This is true as a matter of principle. In fact, it is obvious. It is a closed system. In a similar vein, money is the fluid in the market cycle (which is why people of finance talk about the "liquidity" in the marketplace). If it is not allowed to leak out, the market cycle also forms a closed loop in which the money that shows up in the collective pocket of the consumer matches exactly the aggregate costs incurred by the productive sector in bringing its products to market.

In a hydraulic loop, there is no particular action required to keep it running smoothly except to insure that the amount of fluid in the system is maintained at the right level. Likewise, there is no particular manipulation of the market cycle required to keep it running smoothly, except to insure that the quantity of currency the in monetary stream is maintained at the level needed to service the demands of trade.

If, however, the hydraulic loop springs a leak, then a way must be found to continually add fluid to keep the circulating stream from dropping too low (which would cause stress in and damage to the system), or even going dry (leading to final breakdown). If the leak is such that its flow erodes the breach over time and makes it larger, this task of keeping the loop supplied will become increasingly difficult, until at some point it becomes virtually impossible, and the system dries up and breaks down anyway irregardless of how much fluid one pours in.

Looking at our market cycle, if its monetary fluid finds a way to leak out, its level too will drop too low (causing stress and damage to both producer and consumer), and eventually dry up (leading to economic depression, and eventual collapse). Such leakage does in fact now occur in the form of the "interest" payments, which are effectively subtracted from the flow of the system between the production and consumption stages, and are therefore no longer available to purchase already produced goods. The only way to prevent the market cycle from running low on circulating currency, and then breaking down, is to continually bring more money into circulation.

The way this is done within the current system is by people in the economy borrowing more money from the banking system; i.e. taking on more "debt". This is not a simple matter of replacement, however, because the current banking practice of charging "interest" on a <u>compounding</u> basis causes the leakage due to "interest" payments to grow over time. People feel obliged to work at an ever-increasing pace to "grow" the economy, but at some point it becomes impossible to keep up. The system runs dry, and then economic machinery slows down, and eventually grinds to a halt. In this case, of course, we are not talking about ruining mere machinery, but human lives.

The obvious way that a leaky hydraulic loop might be kept going is to put a tub under the leak, and recycle the fluid through a pipeline that transfers it back to a point where it can reenter the loop. Similarly, in the market cycle there is a sort of tub that is placed under the monetary leakage that catches it, from where the lost currency can be returned to circulation, thereby becoming available to buy back the equivalent of what it represents in production (thus completing the market cycle).

This tub can be visualized in the form of the personal accounts of those wealthy investors who are privileged to hold portfolios of stocks, bonds, mortgages and other debt instruments. The "interest" payments on these "investment vehicles" are effectively collected into the accounts (the tubs) of those holding them. The net effect of this is to transfer monetary wealth from those who need it to pay their bills, to those who do not. This creates a veritable monetary pipeline from the working poor, middle class and productive entrepreneurs to the passive holders of excess financial wealth.

Of course, these prosperous folk are consumers also, and they could spend or gift their largess back into the circulating currency stream where it would become available to complete the production-consumption cycle. Indeed, sometimes they do, in the form of lavish spending on luxury goods, or through philanthropic gifting. But, there has arisen in this nation, and increasingly the world, a culture of making-money-with-money which makes it seem that the prudent, reasonable, or even moral course to take is to roll-over these excess funds into yet more "investments". After all, why should one give one's own money away; did one not take a "risk" in "earning" it; are there not other people asking for these funds; by "re-investing" are they not providing needed access to them? Within the ambience of such a "culture", those who are the recipients of "interest" payments on debt will be inclined to withhold from the market cycle the proceeds from their gain, until, that is, someone offers to "borrow" it from them, at which point it will reenter production-consumption loop at the price of a yet higher net interest charge against the money supply. This, in turn, will divert ever greater amounts of money into the "tubs" of "investors".

This interest-receipt/re-loaning/interest-payment cycle is a compounding spiral that is driving the tendency for a growing gap between the middle-class-&-poor and the privileged (as opposed to entrepreneurial) rich; the earn-money and the have-money elements of the social order. In the end it will co-opt virtually all healthy flow in the economy itself. No amount of income redistribution will redress this imbalance. Equity can only be achieved when the franchise for money creation and issuance is removed from the private banking sector and restored to the public domain.

A Necessary Caveat:

All the above notwithstanding, it is at this juncture important to state that this tome is not a blanket proscription against the making of investments, loaning at interest, the accumulation of wealth, or the practice of private banking. Indeed, when performed in the right way in appropriate circumstances, these are necessary and noble undertakings. Financial stewardship can be a right-livelihood, and indeed a high calling. My purpose is to open up a cogent discussion in this area; not presume to pronounce over it any final dispensation or judgment. The practice of private banks loaning money at interest for private enterprise (as has long been the practice of savings-&-loan associations and credit unions) is not the crux of the problem. Nor is the problem investment per se. On the contrary, the existence of mechanisms for the accumulation of privately-stewarded capital is a necessary and productive aspect of the free enterprise system. Investment money, however, should be just that; i.e. money for productive investment. It should <u>not</u> be a mechanism for borrowing the grocery money back into circulation, or for making up for the inability of producers to obtain a parity price for their wares, because the citizenry and its elected leaders have neglected their civic and moral responsibility to insure that a money supply adequate to complete the market cycle in its own domestic economy is issued.

In an outward sense, the root of the problem is the practice of allowing private banks to create money with the stroke of a pen via an ostensible "loan" process, and attaching to its principal proceeds a compounding "interest" charge. By this, a sovereign power that belongs rightly and necessarily to the commonweal has been usurped as a private franchise. Because this practice creates a situation whereby the national economy as a whole cannot complete its production-&-consumption cycle without descending ever further into "debt" to an amorphous extra-national entity, our supposedly sovereign nation in its entirety is relegated to the de facto status of a business in the portfolio of an extra-national corporation. What is worse, it is obliged to conduct its business in the throes of an ongoing bankruptcy reorganization. Within such a monetization scheme, "investment" that is not truly investment becomes the norm, and the culture within which it occurs is pervasively contorted to rationalize the practice.

There is a solution to this conundrum: that is, for *We the People* to re-assert our sovereign power to create, issue and regulate money itself. The natural vehicle for us to achieve this end at present is our government. This, to be perfectly clear, is not to say that we need government to "meddle in business". On the contrary, it is the key to finally getting government out of the meddling game. The very word "government" has become a pejorative in large part due to the long litany of abuses that have been perpetrated through its "good offices". I would assert, however, that our estrangement from this arm of our collective volition would begin to be healed if it were redeemed from being the agency of a corrupt monetary principle, and restored as an accountable executor of the common will. What is more, the whole financial house within which we do business would be renovated from being a speculative casino in which the only viable strategy is to get in, make a killing, and get out, to one in which the practice of investment was genuine, open-ended and productive. Such salutary change in the financial zeitgeist would play out in ways that would be truly transformative on many levels.

This leads naturally to a very big discourse that there is not space for here. It behooves us to suspend the usual judgments on the subject of money long enough to explore that discourse. Within the current paradigm, the mathematical inanity, lack of transparency and venal character of the monetary order makes any profound realization, reckoning and rectification with respect to government impossible. But, if in our hearts and minds we can make the transformative leap on the subject of money and government, then we will not have merely re-formed the same old noxious system, but transported its taproot to fresh new earth. The saving grace in this whole situation is that both the cause of, and the solution to, our monetary straits are eminently cognizable. Indeed, it must be so at this providential juncture. If humankind persists in its denial on this wise and continues lemming-like over the "debt-money" cliff, it will have done so with "eyes wide shut".

The problems that have proliferated out of the current monetary order have become complex virtually beyond human reckoning. Notwithstanding, this Gordian knot can be cut by returning the basis of the system to sound principle. So, how can this be done? The heart of the answer, of course, lies within each of us. From an outer perspective the crux of returning to sound principle will be the restoration of the monetary power to the public domain. This will not be the end of economic history, but a new beginning. From there the dialogue on all issues will unfold in ways that are scarcely imaginable now, and a vast new frontier of human possibilities will be revealed.

CHAPTER 2
THE SIX STAGES OF COPING

Summation of the Monetary Problem:

Within the present system, money is "loaned" into existence through a private banking system with a compounding "interest" fee attached, but the monetary credits necessary to "pay back" this "interest" are not issued. Practically speaking, the only way the economy can be maintained with an adequate money supply, while allowing the people to pay their bills and consume their own production, is to continually "borrow" ever- greater sums of money at a compounding rate from private banks. Unless this is changed as the operative principle by which money is created, issued and controlled, virtually all tangible assets in the nation will be effectively confiscated through default, the social order will be destroyed, and the earth itself will be ruined.

The Six Stages of Coping:

Within the present "debt"-based monetary system, there are essentially six ways by which the shortchanging of the market cycle caused by the "interest" charge attached to the creation of money are ostensibly addressed, or, more accurately, coped with. In practice these tend to unfold in a progression that generally unfolds as follows:

Stage #1 – "Let the market correct itself"

This is "solution" that is generally promoted actively in the "conservative" philosophies of "free market" ideologues. Allow the "business cycle" to "hit bottom", so the rhetoric goes, and eventually it will "bounce back", if, that is, the government can restrain itself from interfering. In reality, left to its own devices, the market will tend to go through a process that approximates the following:

When people have lost confidence in their economic prospects for the future, their tendency is to cash in the paper "assets" they are holding for whatever they can get, and then concentrate on paying their bills until times get better. As loans are paid off the principal amounts remitted to the banks are extinguished on the banks' books (i.e. the money goes out of existence), thereby reducing the money supply itself. This, in turn, causes a further reduction of economic activity. Over time, this results in a spiraling economic contraction.

The descent into implosion will tend to be slowed by the reality that those "investors" who have bought "debt paper" (i.e. loan contracts) for the privilege of receiving the "interest" payments will have to start spending the proceeds of the payments already received because prospects for "reinvesting" it (i.e. re-lending it out at interest) will diminish to almost zero. With much of the money supply disappearing into the banks, these would-be "investment" funds become an increasingly large portion of the money still in circulation. Eventually those holding them will feel the need to start using them for living expenses. This will reintroduce this pent-up money into circulation, this time without an additional interest charge attached. Still the contraction will go on, as there will be a further shrinkage of the monetary pool as people hold onto their most essential properties (houses, cars, businesses or whatever) by continuing to make payments on the bank loans against them.

Federal Reserve banker John Exter predicted such a scenario when he warned: *"The Fed is locked into this continuing credit expansion. It can't stop. If ever bank lending slows ... the game is up, and the scramble for liquidity starts."* and *"The Fed will be powerless to stop a deflationary collapse once it starts."*

Indeed this "deflationary collapse" has evidently started with the 2008-9 economic crisis. There are some who say we should just let it go and allow the market to correct itself, even if that means enduring another Depression. After all, did we not have one in the '30's, and did we not come out of it fit to fight WWII and emerge as a victorious superpower? There are many factors that are overlooked in such a statement, not the least of which is that the world has changed drastically since the decade of the '30's. We live in an unprecedented era. Among other things, the farms, industries and fundamental skills upon which the nation subsisted during the last Depression have effectively atrophied. There is not much that remains in the way of subsistence capability. For practical purposes we in the "developed world" are no longer living on the land, and therefore there is no land to return to as a refuge for weathering another economic storm. Monetary collapse was horrific last time; it would be unthinkable now.

Stage #2 – "Borrow" More Money

The monetary market can be left to correct itself for only so long. Sooner or later someone, be they private individuals, corporate entities or government, must re-initiate the process of taking on more "debt", or the money supply will drop to zero, literally. If the citizenry can't be inspired to do it, then the government (primarily at the Federal level) will feel virtually forced to step in as the "borrower of last resort". Theoretically, this is what the "bailout packages" have been all about. They are designed to inject "borrowed" money back into the economy to jolt it back into activity. The gambit seems to have stabilized the situation for now (or at least slowed the slide), but clearly it has not been a solution, as even this massive new "stimulus" has not had a big enough effect to get economic activity trending upward again.

There are a number of reasons why this is so, but much of it is rooted in the fact that confidence in future prospects within the present economic regime has been largely destroyed, even amongst bankers (which is why they are so reluctant now to lend even to each other). The ongoing ability and willingness on the part of the citizenry to take on ever greater amounts of "debt" is the very engine of the Federal Reserve monetary scheme, but the fantastic magnitude of the numbers associated with the latest "rescue packages" have effectively dampened any expectation that the effort will result in a new round of "economic growth". When the plan for keeping the economic ship afloat has been reduced to "borrowing" ever greater amounts of money to pay off previously "borrowed" money, plus "interest", as opposed to issuing money based on real production, there is not much to encourage the citizenry to borrow more money. The last remaining engine of "debt"-money expansion, then, is abject necessity, as people resort to re-mortgaging their house, laying down their credit card, visiting the payday lender, and other financial survival techniques to get money for gas, groceries and critical bills.

Stage #3 – Call for the Government to "Balance Its Budget"

Caught between the prospects of a collapsing money supply and a galloping "indebtedness", and lacking any effective consciousness of the monetary taproot of the economic problem, those in positions of social, political or economic leadership search for a more nuanced position by which they can wiggle through the present crisis. This results in endless pontificating in the public discourse about the need for government to finally "conduct itself like a business", "cut its spending", and "balance its budgets". This is, effectively, a rhetorical tap dance that tries to straddle the opposing "necessities" of, on one hand, avoiding going hat-in-hand to the banking system for more funds by firing people and shrinking the economy, and, on the other, for someone (government or private) to go to the banking system to take on enough new "debt" to prime the economic pump so those people can be hired back again; all while money is being lost from the monetary pool at a compounding rate due to the leakage caused by having to make "interest" payments on every dollar in circulation. There is no conceivable nuance of taxing, spending and other policy parameters that can prevent an arrangement founded on such utter illogic from failing. To think otherwise is to imagine that a one-hundred gallon tub can be made full with fifty gallons of water simply because one can get water to rise to the rim here and there by a fury of churning. The effort is all fuss and froth, but the basic parameters of the proposition are wholly flawed.

No one wants be the party to take on more debt, so behind virtually all personal, social and political contentions there lurks an effective agenda to clear one's own debts, and oblige someone else to take on the burden. The citizenry expects the government to take care of them through hard economic times (while "balancing the budget", of course), while our public servants try (amidst much hand-wringing about having to "balance the budget") to pass the onus back to the citizenry (the people need to "make sacrifices"). The corporate sector attempts to recoup enough liquidity to float its own financial ship by inflating the prices of its products, while consumer activists wax outraged at corporate greed. The mavens of finance, academia and media weigh in with their own expert obfuscations. Saturation advertising induces consumers to slide unmindfully into debt to maintain lifestyles, and keep up with the Joneses. For the most part, we don't think about our affairs this way, but the engine of "debt" is always there subconsciously driving every fact of our lives, including how we think, how we feel and how we act. The consequences are immersive.

The long and short of the situation is that, within an economic regime financed by privately-issued, "debt"-based money with a compounding "interest" fee attached, there is no conceivable combination of factors that could allow for the closing of the production-consumption loop in the private sector, the balancing of budgets in the public sector, and the prevention of the whole societal enterprise from sliding into irredeemable "debt" to those interests that control the creation, issuance and control of the money (save by the improbably altruistic deed of everyone who benefits from such an arrangement gifting their thus-gained surplus back to society so that the money stays in circulation and "indebtedness" does not snowball).

The upshot of all this, it seems, is that another way has to be found to find the money to simultaneously complete the private market cycle and balance government budgets. If the money can't be found within the domestic economy, then perhaps it can be found outside of it.

Stage #4 – Try for a "Positive Balance" in International Trade

The fourth stage in attempting to solve the U.S. economic riddle is to try to earn the monetary credits lost through "interest" payments by achieving a positive balance-of-payments account with its "trading partners"; that is, by selling more to our international trading partners than we buy from them so we can keep the extra money. This notion overlooks the critical fact that the national currencies of every other nation on earth have the same fatal flaw as the U.S. dollar: that is, they are created and issued via loans from private banks. This means that our foreign brethren also lack the ability to close their own domestic market cycles without resorting constantly to taking on more "debt". The logic of their situation, then, compels them to take advantage of their trading partners, including the U.S. economy, to financially survive. It is impossible, of course, for every nation on earth to beggar every other nation, and so in the domestic political life of each, recriminations inevitably ensue about the "unfairness" of foreign trading partners that does not allow one's own folk to recoup their own just due. The impossibility of trade equity manifesting in a world where the trading order is structurally a less-than-zero sum game almost never seems to occur to anyone. The problem is tantamount to having a tub where one's own liquidity is leaking out at a compounding rate, and then blaming everyone else, who, it happens, is experiencing the same problem, instead of finding and remedying the common reason for the respective leakages. Lacking such a coming to one's senses, the de facto reality is that the seeming net "indebtedness" of the world to the extra-national private banking system, and now extra-national corporations, is, in the aggregate, being driven up virtually without regard for other factors. In the end, this is a lose-lose- lose- lose- lose- ... scenario for all peoples.

None of these coping strategies are satisfactory as solutions. They may offer temporary relief here and there, but in the end only tend to compound the problems of the system. They are the very roads to unintended consequences.

Stage #5 – Allow a Limited Wave of "Bankruptcies"

As the economy as a whole slides into unsupportable "debt", there will inevitably come a time when a wave of bankruptcies will begin to occur. This will generally be followed by a spate of hand wringing in the public discourse warning that this phenomenon poses a threat to the viability of the economy. There is an element of truth in this, in that the publicity surrounding such a wave of defaults will undermine confidence in the economy, thereby discouraging people from going to the banks to "borrow" more money. From a strictly monetary perspective, however, bankruptcies are the safety valve of the "debt"-based monetary system.

When someone who has taken out a bank loan goes bankrupt, most "debt" contracts against any money he has "borrowed" from a commercial bank and spent into circulation are generally cancelled (there are exceptions), but the principal sum remains in circulation. This means that the amount of money in circulation remains unchanged by the bankruptcy, but the size of the "debt" obligation it is obliged to support is reduced. As "interest" payments are made, this "debt" obligation, and more, will be incurred again, but the bankruptcy allows for a period of respite.

While a wave of bankruptcies can, in a manner of speaking, be accommodated, the numbers cannot be allowed to spiral out of control. This means that the officials who control monetary policy find themselves in the position of having to walk a line between causing the injection of more money, or less, into the economy. If it allows relatively more, the economy will revive and confidence, theoretically, will be restored, but at the price of taking on still more "debt". If it opts for relatively less, the number of bankruptcies will be greater, but a measure of the "debt" load carried by the money supply will be reduced for now, and into the future. Neither course, however, provides any real solution to the monetization problem.

The issue of more or less money injection is not the only concern. It is inevitable that any policy adopted will affect the matter of which participants in the economy will be obliged to absorb the brunt of personal trauma that attends bankruptcy. In this ongoing economic crisis, it appears that policy makers have opted, for the most part, to bail out the fortunes of "Wall Street", while letting "Main Street" take the hit. This has led, as might be expected, to much heated debate about both the moral equity and the economic veracity of the road taken. It should be noted that either way there would have been negative effects, and still no solution to the basic monetary dysfunction that caused the seeming inevitability of this desperate measure as an economic remedy to begin with.

Stage #6 – Restarting the Economy via "War" and "Sub-Prime Lending"

While the pressure on the economy from so-called monetary "debt" can be relieved for a time by a wave of bankruptcies, ultimately the economy cannot be sustained by this phenomenon. Sooner or later the vanishing money supply must be replenished. This means that at some point (despite mounting reasons to distrust "the system") someone must be willing to go back to the banking system and reinstitute "borrowing" money on a massive scale. This can be done either by individuals and corporations in the private sector, or by government in the public. The question then becomes, how can the private and/or political will necessary to bring that about be mustered, given the factors enumerated above that work increasingly against such an occurrence?

Historically, the answer to such an impasse has been to find a war to get involved in. Its effect is to stir up the emotion of the citizenry to such a pitch that people are willing to forgo their qualms that hold sway in the coping stages enumerated above. When there is an enemy, real or imagined, that threatens the very existence of one's family, nation and sacred way of life, do not worries about "debt" become trivial?

These "wars" can take different forms. The most obvious is the "hot war," which is a military contest with a foreign state. It can also be a "cold war" against a rival. Increasingly, it has manifested as a "simmering war" against an enemy who threatens our "domestic security." These "wars" can also be social in their focus, such as in the "war on poverty," "war on drugs," "war against AIDS," and so forth. Monetarily speaking, the particular nature of the "war" is secondary to the fact that it motivates the society to start "borrowing" money again.

In the past, "war" as an agent of "debt" creation was the most common mode of overcoming "debt" phobia. Until the mid-twentieth century, the world still had geographically defined economic frontiers, and so "hot wars" were the way to go, but within an economic production and trading matrix that has gone global and become intimately interconnected, they do too much damage to the socio/political/economic house. In a nuclear age it has become reckless to pick fights between major states, but the hot-war technique can still be employed in a limited way if the perception of "the enemy" can be isolated to defenseless "rogue states," or people holed up in caves in some remote mountains.

Since WWII, "cold war" has been the stimulus of choice, but with the collapse of the Soviet Empire a new rival has had to be concocted. For America, the leading candidate for this role is, it seems, an "emerging" China. Still, the specter of a second "superpower" has not sufficiently coalesced to warrant the levels of military spending necessary to sustain the economy's appetite for "debt" money, so a "simmering" war on a largely amorphous "terrorist threat" has stepped in as the military exigency of last resort.

On the domestic front, the social "wars" have been largely disparaged politically as "socialism" or "wasteful liberal spending". This factor is making a bid to be revived with the proposed legislation for national health care, but that has not yet manifested. To be sure, much social spending continues in the form of Social Security, Medicare and "welfare payments."

Since WWII, another generator of "debt" has been spending on infrastructure. This has been spearheaded largely by government, as it sought to provide what the political establishment saw as necessary elements of the commons for a burgeoning nation. One item of note was the interstate highway system, a massive public work whose ripple effect caused a commensurate investment in private infrastructure around these city-connecting and city-center-bypassing corridors. There were also large investments by industry in updated productive capacities, though this factor was attenuated early-on by the inexorable crumbling of the traditional "rustbelt" industries.

In the private economy the primary engine of money-creation has been consumer "debt." Through the early part of the post-WWII period this factor revolved around the ballooning demand for consumer goods, fueled largely by the need to outfit Baby Boomers and their parents in their migration to the suburbs, as expedited by the interstate highway system. As the decades progressed, the factor that came to the fore was the "housing bubble." At length, even this boom could not be sustained, but the phenomenon had become such a crucial vehicle for ongoing "economic growth" (read "debt-money creation") that we of this culture, buyers and financiers alike, did not know how to reign in the resulting orgy of speculation. The game was stretched beyond supportable limits with the sub-prime lending phenomenon.

It should be noted here that the "sub-prime lending crisis" did not bring down the economy. Rather it stretched out the pyramid scheme represented by the "fractional reserve" monetary regime by effectively sacrificing people as the price for "borrowing" more money into the economy to make compounding "interest" payments on old bank loans. When "unqualified borrowers" defaulted after a time on their payments, the money they failed to "pay back" remained in circulation, but the "debt" against the portion of the money supply it represented was lifted. From the perspective of the economy as a whole, this became "debt"-free money, and it continues to circulate to the benefit of everyone. Indeed, it may be fairly argued that without the net injection of funds unburdened by "interest" via "sub-prime lending" practices (however scurrilous), the crisis we are experiencing now in the economy would have precipitated years ago.

The bizarre reality of our current predicament is that, far from being the sources of financial "costs" that are bankrupting the nation, such economically dubious enterprises as sub-prime lending and wars in the Middle East are not the reasons that we cannot, supposedly, afford domestically to build infrastructure, hire teachers and provide for universal health care. On the contrary, they have functioned as the cash-cows for the "financial liquidity" (i.e. currency) needed to keep the economy afloat so that the money necessary to pay for infrastructure, teachers and health care is available at all. None of this is to be construed to mean that enterprise that is inimical to human life, such as wars and mortgage swindles, are somehow necessary elements of a healthy economy. Rather, it is a telling indicator that, monetarily speaking, we as a nation have descended into such madness that these dubious enterprises have come somehow to constitute the economics of last resort.

One area where private citizens are still taking on a burgeoning "debt" is in student loans, but this source of cash will also get tapped out and remain as a crushing residual burden on the populace.

In the meantime, the numbers associated with "debt" have reached such staggering proportions that even the military and social wars combined, have grown to be inadequate for providing the margin of liquidity needed to float the economic ship. Ergo, there has arisen the "necessity" for "troubled assets" (essentially worthless paper) bailout programs. These have injected massive amounts of freshly "borrowed" money into the economy, but because they are so far removed from any real basis in new wealth creation that could justify them as collateral, confidence in the monetary system, including amongst bankers and others who work in finance, has been largely destroyed. In more rational economic times, these "toxic assets" would have been permitted to fail, thereby causing a lifting of a massive increment of the "debt" burden against the money supply. Had we as a nation exercised sufficient collective wit and courage to forebear this initiative, it would likely (the prospect is not certain, since the economy relies in the end on myriad human factors) have given the economy a new lease on life, but we as a culture (the problem is by no means only limited to bankers and politicians) have become so addicted to the illusion of "debt"-based financing as the basis for our "economic security" that we no longer have enough objective distance from the monetary problem that is ruining our lives to see it.

That is the bad news. The good news is that a solution to the monetary crisis is only a wake-up call away, assuming, of course, that we can rouse ourselves out of our individual and collective monetary comas.

Taking the Beam Out of One's Own Eye
I would hasten to point out that the stages of monetary dysfunction as given above are a product of our culture, and not a function of any person, or class of persons, appearances to the contrary notwithstanding. We are all, in our own ways and niches, parts of the problem and potential agents for the cure. The Biblical injunction to take the beam out of our own eye before attempting to remove the mote out of our brother's eye has never been more apt. We need dialogue and understanding, not recrimination and confrontation, to deal with this all-pervasive social matter.

The Threefold Solution

There is a threefold solution to the economic conundrum, but it is one that has not yet been consciously tried in the world. To be sure, elements of it have found their way into the economic life from time to time, but for the most part such developments have been desultory, incomplete and unconscious. My intention for the rest of this treatise is to bring what is required to a clarity of consciousness. Before embarking on such a delineation, however, it is necessary to identify and name the three basic domains of a natural threefold economic life:

(1) – The Cultural Economy
(2) – The National Economy
(3) – The Global Economy

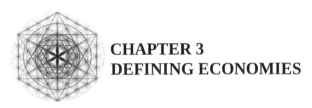

CHAPTER 3
DEFINING ECONOMIES

The Cultural, National & Global Economies:

What is commonly referred to as "the economy" is in actuality a three-part construct, and for purposes of this discussion it would be useful to identify and name a domain associated with each. These are, respectively:

- The Cultural Economy – This is what a conventional economist would associate with the "micro-economy." It embodies the economic activities of individuals and their institutional proxies (i.e. businesses, families, foundations, associations, state and local governments, etc.). It is a term which describes the vastly diverse "players" in the economy. One way or another it includes everyone, individually and in all their associations, whether in the capacity of producers or consumers.

- The National Economy - This is what a conventional economist would associate with the "macro-economy," and it identifies the national domestic economy as a whole. It is set up by the body of law that defines how the "monetary system" operates; particularly the way in which money is created, issued and controlled. In the American system, the responsibility for this function is assigned constitutionally to the Federal government. There is a commonly held misconception which assumes that the Federal government is a "business", and must therefore be run according to sound business principles (one can hear this on the political stump and in the media more-or-less constantly). Properly speaking, businesses are participants in the cultural economy because they do not have the authority to create money (that is, they have the legal and moral authority to represent only themselves, and not the whole nation). The Federal government, on the other hand, <u>is</u> the agent for national sovereignty, and, accordingly, does have the authority to issue money (which is the most pervasive element of the commons). The Federal government is <u>NOT, NOT, NOT</u> a "business", and to even think that it could be run as one is a corruption. Monetarily speaking, businesses serve private profit, at the expense of the whole (even if in reality its work is of benefit to the whole, which indeed it often is), but the Federal government by definition serves the commonweal. It is, ideally, the political representative of the sovereign national-economic entity within which cultural-economic enterprises such as businesses operate (notwithstanding, that the national economy of the U.S. has de facto become a business in the portfolio of privileged financial interests due to the abdication by our elected representatives in the Federal government of their money-creation power to an extra-national banking cartel).

- Global-Economy – In the language of economics it would be logical to call the economy of the world as a whole the "meta-economy" ("meta" meaning transcendent of the whole), although I have almost never heard such a phrase used in conventional economic discourse. In a simple material sense it can be considered to be an aggregate concept, consisting of the sum total of all the cultural and national economic activity that makes up the whole global economy. From a higher perspective, however, it is a transcendent idea, because the economic activities that occur materially within the unity of the whole don't simply add up arithmetically, but interact with each other to create a compounding array of new connections, possibilities, identities and meanings.

Given these three domains, it follows that the economic order calls for a threefold answer to remedy its defects. These can be identified as:

(1) – The Cultural Economic Zeitgeist (CEZ)
(2) – The National Economic Picture (NEP)
(3) – The Global Economic Matrix (GEM)

The Cultural Economic Zeitgeist (CEZ):

At the very root of the economic life lies a fundamental question about the nature and purpose of money. It might be stated as – "Is it the purpose of life to serve money, or the purpose of money to serve life?" or - "Will money be used selfishly in the spirit of personal gain, or altruistically for the greater good?" Which attitude is adopted will determine the character of culture that grows up around monetary ideals, which in turn guides monetary praxis. Let us make no mistake. This is a stark choice, and any tendency to come to a "nuanced" position will be unfruitful, self-deceptive and ultimately counterproductive. Upon this question the entire economic conundrum turns, and it rests squarely with the individual to make the determination.

This is not to say that we can never find occasion to use money to provide our personal needs or satisfy our personal desires. Rather, it speaks to the spirit out of which any use of this all-pervasive and powerful artifact of the social order will be employed. There is a word of German origin that has no direct counterpart in the English language, and has increasingly been adopted in our culture to express a spirit that could not otherwise be so accurately expressed. It is "zeitgeist," which is defined by Webster's dictionary as "the general intellectual, moral, and cultural climate of an era". For purposes of this dissertation I would define it more concisely yet as being "the spiritual ambiance of any culture in its own time". The zeitgeist of our time, then, is the spiritual ground out of which our culture germinates, which in turn determines everything about what the civilization that grows from it comes to be and do. One can take this assertion religiously, metaphorically, philosophically or even materially in the most rigorous sense, and, I would suggest, it still holds true.

The fundamental problem with our economy is that at its root it grows out of a spirit that is not congruent with the needs of our time. We as a civilization have largely abandoned any concerted search for such out of a modern utilitarian spirit rooted in personal gain. Ultimately this will render the economic life incapable of supplying even our own personal needs. At worse, it will destroy the social fabric and render the earth sterile.

In a practical sense a decision for the higher path will mean that people will be a great deal more disposed to look out for the needs of "the-other", as opposed to their own. This may sound more that a bit idealistic, though we often act privately in this spirit even now. It will become far more prevalent as the social norm when the fear of lack is obviated by the transparency, directness and sufficiency of an economic order that does not use as its life's blood a currency issued as "debt" burdened with an "interest" payment, which is really a fee or tribute attached to the creation, issuance and control of money by private parties who have been given control of society's own monetary powers.

That said, we should not imagine that it is the greed of the bankers as a group that is responsible for this mess. Indeed, I have come to know many of them, and as a rule they are as fine (and, truth be told, as flawed) a category of people as one could expect to find in any walk of life. I would pose the question, if the bankers are getting all the money for creating the currency out of thin air, and receiving "interest" payments for every dollar of that sum, why are so many banks going bankrupt themselves? There are detailed and comprehensive answers for this, but there is not room to do the question justice in this short piece. Suffice it to say for now that banking is a tightly controlled profession, and bankers as people have surprisingly little (though I don't say "no") latitude for acting independently to control how they do their business. This is true to a surprising extent even for those that appear to control the system.

The zeitgeist of this era is rooted in a spirit of expediency that has resulted in our economic life unfolding as a tyranny of numbers that virtually all aspects of life are obliged to serve. This is so even for those that, one might imagine, are the core conspirators for the present order. The monster has gotten away from them also, as money has taken on a life of its own. There is no one who has intended this as an end. In a human sense, then, it is in the interest of all of us, from the most destitute denizen of the hinterland, to the czars of financial affairs at the top of the Manhattan towers, to adopt a spirit with respect to money that sees it as a means to the common good. Therein resides for every one of us our essential vested interest.

CHAPTER 4
THE ROLE OF GOVERNMENT

Defining the National Economic Picture (NEP)

The National Economic Picture (NEP) is the image of economic activity a society visualizes itself altogether as doing. It consists of two mirrored pictures.

The first, the "material/human picture", is a primary image of the actual material and human resources that are available to perform whatever tasks the nation sees as needful or desirable to be done, specifically as regards to the coming year. The year in question could be a Gregorian calendar year, or, alternately, a sort of "fiscal year" by which the beginning and ending of such an annual period would be reckoned (It seems to me most natural to demarcate it from winter solstice to winter solstice since that most organically bookends the natural rhythms of the earth, in the northern hemisphere at least).

The second, the "monetization picture", is a reflection of the material/human picture in monetary terms, which will, in turn, be used to guide the money creation, issuance and control process by which life will be breathed into the material/human economy. The resulting monetary emission will act as an economic leaven that facilitates the interaction of the material and human elements represented in the NEP through the economic activities of trading, loaning and gifting. Outwardly it would resemble the "fiscal budgeting" process that Congress employs at present, except the monetization picture is <u>not</u> a delineation of what we as a nation can "afford" to do within the constrains of available tax receipts supplemented by the ability to "borrow" more money, but rather a tabulation of the amount and mode of issue of newly-created money that will be required to activate the material/human economy envisioned.

In a limited sense, the monetization process can be thought of as akin to how play money is issued to facilitate the board game *Monopoly*. One can think of the picture presented by the board itself as a monetization picture for which money needs to be issued to play the game. I can imagine that at some point, presumably after the design of the board was determined, the designers were faced with the question of how much money would need to be made available to the game, and according to what modes and timings. to maximize the ability of each player to play to his potential, while maintaining an even hand with respects to the interests of each. To be sure, the *Monopoly* analogy is limited in that the game itself is designed to bring out the competitive impulse to the extent that one player will in the end vanquish all the rest, while in the game of life the purpose would be to encourage a self-regulating cooperative order. How this is facilitated will become evident as this dissertation unfolds.

The power to "monetize" the economy (i.e. create the money to activate actual economic enterprise) proceeds out of the Constitutional duty of the Federal government to create a supply of money to facilitate whatever commerce would naturally be performed by the people of the nation as a whole (as private individuals, corporate entities and governmental bodies), as guided by its stated mission to *"promote the general Welfare"*. The division of responsibility for this task breaks down into three parts, according to the respective branches of government.

It is the duty of the <u>Legislative Branch</u>, in accordance with the Constitutionally delegated power of Congress *"to coin Money [and] regulate the Value thereof"*, to enact legislation that authorizes the creation of the dollars that are the life's blood of the nation's economy. The process starts with the drawing up a monetization picture. This would constitute essentially the formulation of an estimate for the coming year based on the material and human resources available to the country, and a general picture of how this might be employed in the context of the social will. Much of this would, of course, be predicated on the record of what transpired in the previous year, but the process also entails great potential and promise for guiding the development of the country into the future.

This may sound like a tall order, but the Federal Reserve already performs a similar function. They are obliged to do so as a basis for implementing monetary policy. The root problem within the current system is that this task is not performed in service to the true welfare of the people, but is largely dictated by usury-based financial demands of "investors". Its "projections" are not for the most part based upon human needs, but on the pseudo-need for money to "earn" money in speculative financial markets. This was made starkly evident in the recent round of "economic rescue packages" which were heavily weighted towards the bailing out of banks and financial markets, at the neglect of reforming the monetary system itself so that that the people who produce the tangible wealth of the country would be fairly compensated for their work. To be sure, there were many cries for increased regulation, but "regulation" will not fix the basic flaw at the heart of the monetary system, which is the issuance of the money supply privately, at "interest". It is easy to criticize bankers and politicians for their venality (critiques which are in some measure warranted), but within the present "debt"-money culture and consequent system, they are largely constrained form acting otherwise. (This is a topic that sorely needs discussion, but there is not room to do it justice in this short treatise).

The monetization process would commence in the lower chamber of the legislature in the spirit conveyed by *"All Bills for raising Revenue shall originate in the House of Representatives"* (Art 1, Sec 7, Para 1), and be ratified in consultation with the Senate. The result would be in the form of legislation expressed in terms that could be put into motion via the "spending" or "loaning" of publicly-created money.

It is the duty of the <u>Executive Branch</u> to perform the tasks necessary to create and dispense the money required to financially actualize the legislation passed. This process would be guided by the monetization picture. It would most decidedly not be the Treasury's job to legislate, but they may bring in skills necessary to formulate, interpret and facilitate the monetization mandate. The Secretary of the Treasury would be charged with overseeing the day-to-day conduct of monetary policy, much as the chairman of the Fed does now, except that he would be operating within socially conscious guidelines stipulated via legislation, instead of the financial dictates of the speculative money markets.

The role of the <u>Judicial Branch</u> is to oversee the equity of the whole process in the context of the Constitution. It is possible that the Supreme Court might even be the body that initiates the transition to public monetization. The question of the Constitutionality of the Federal Reserve System has, as far as I am aware, never come to the docket of the nation's supreme tribunal, but, in the words of Congressman Wright Patman from Texas, former chairman of the House Banking and Currency Committee:

"The monetary powers . . . are reserved to the Congress by the Constitution. . . . But it is not within the Congress' constitutional means to delegate these powers without proscribing policy

objectives and clear guidelines detailing how these powers may be used (i.e. legislation guiding their use). Inevitably the Supreme Court has held as unconstitutional those grants of powers made without any spelling out of the specific objectives and limitations placed on their use. . . . There is little doubt in the author's mind that if any legal challenge were ever raised to the Federal Reserve's monetary policies, the courts would hold them unconstitutional."

Chairman Patman's point was sharpened in an illustrative exchange between Bruce Spence, chairman of the House Banking and Currency Committee, and William McChesney Martin, chairman of the Fed, in a hearing related to the *Financial Institutions Act of 1957*, that went as follows:

Chairman Spence: *When we delegate power to an agency, without any standards or limitations or definitions or restrictions, it is a legislative power that we delegate.*
Mr. Martin: *That is what I conceive . . .*
Chairman Spence: *We have delegated that to the Federal Reserve.*
Mr. Martin: *That is correct, sir.*
Chairman Spence: *Without restrictions or standards.*
Mr. Martin: *Oh, yes indeed.*

What Backs the Money?

Confidence in the image people hold of the viability of the economy it represents is always, in the final analysis, the "backing for" (i.e. willingness to accept) any currency; all the apotheoses of precious metals, "eligible paper" (i.e. collateral for "debt"), or "financial indicators" notwithstanding. To be sure, this has rarely been a very precise or conscious process, but it must become so if humankind is ever to break free from being slaves to money, and ultimately liberate its full potential. What is needed, then, is a fully conscious money-creation process that is guided by a mental picture of what the nation as a whole needs, desires, and has the political will to do, based upon the actual availability of material and human resources. The reality-based "material/human picture" comes first, and a money creation assessment, or "monetization picture", is derived from that.

Working on the Building

Permit me to illustrate how this would work. Suppose one felt the need to construct a building. The purpose for the building would be defined, and one would then begin to form an image in one's mind of the edifice required to fulfill it. The next step is to make that image more visible and materially defined. Architectural plans would be drawn up, along with illustrations and construction details. The material and human resources available to bring it into being would be roughly estimated. Bills of materials would be compiled. Contractors would be contacted. Finally this would all be resolved into a tabulated estimate of costs that would be the basis for determining how much money would need to be created and issued (which is precisely what the banker does when he writes the check for the "loan") to carry it out. Summarized succinctly, this monetization picture of the project stated in terms of "costs" is what would be presented to the banker as "eligible paper" (documentation for collateral) for his possible approval as the basis for a "loan" (i.e. the creation of money via an account entry on the bank's books) to "monetize" the project (i.e. give it a monetary dimension so the building can be built).

Now, transpose this same process to the national level. The Congress would fulfill its mandate *"To coin Money (and) regulate the Value thereof"* by creating the "material/human picture" of whatever legislative proposal it deemed to be worthy of creating the funds to finance. It would then compile a "monetization picture" by which it would estimate the "cost" of such a proposal. The aggregate of all such material/human and monetization pictures in any given year would constitute the National Economic Picture. This could include everything from funding highway construction, to paying out for social services, to purchasing arms for national defense, to paying the soldiers to fire them off, and so forth; i.e. the gamut of the work and needs financed by the Federal government. This process would be expedited by Congressional hearings, letters and petitions from constituents, research performed by legislative assistants, and other avenues of democratic input.

In short, the legislative process would take place much in the manner that it does now, but with a critical difference. The dark cloud hanging over the proceedings in the form of the common assumption that there is only so much money to go around, and so we as a nation can only do so much (despite clearly having the material and human means to do more), would be dispelled. It would be replaced by the objective assurance that adequate funds could be issued to finance any conceivable picture of whatever the nation was willing and able to do with the actual material and human resources available, all without incurring any "debt" whatsoever to the nation as a whole.

Gone would be the illogical notion that this nation cannot "afford" to do the things that it clearly has the actual resources on hand to do, and willingness to perform. Absent also would be the budgetary religion that there was some whopping "interest" on a supposed "debt" that would have to be satisfied before we could even begin to think about supplying our needs. This would all take place within the consciousness that the actual productive enterprise of *We the People* is always its own backing for the money issued to finance it.

This process resembles the Congressional "budgeting process" as currently conceived, but properly speaking the word "budget" is a business term that applies to an enterprise for which a source of income has to be found in order to meet expenses. The national economy is, ideally, not a business. It is, rather, a sovereign economic entity within which businesses operate (notwithstanding that it has effectively come to be a business in the portfolio of financial speculators due to the abdication by the Federal government to an extra-national banking cabal of its monetary franchise). It a misnomer to use the term "budget" in the context of an economic enterprise, such as the Federal government, that doesn't need income to monetize its actions. I would suggest that identifying it as a "monetization picture" would be more descriptive, and help to prevent any confusion of the fundamental nature of the process that the Congress is engaged in from creeping back in.

Before leaving the topic, I would add an important clarification. While the Federal government is essentially a political body, it does embody aspects that partake of the nature of a business, and therefore are amenable to business disciplines. The various governmental departments, for example, have their respective missions to perform, but no independent authority to create their own money to fulfill them. In a sense they have to find a "customer" for their work, albeit that the candidates for such a role may be limited to their Congressional or Presidential patrons. In human terms the Federal government is in fact a huge amalgam of individuals and associations who do indeed embody diverse elements of the social, political and economic realms, but none of this is to negate the defining national (macro-economic) characteristic of the Federal government that makes it the natural trustee of the money-creation franchise. It behooves us to be rigorous in our thinking about government, and refrain from indulging in sweeping emotional and ideological generalizations that can only produce dogmatism, conflict and dissolution.

Once the monetization picture was enacted as legislation it would be passed on to the Executive Branch, which would, true to its title, "execute" it. This task would be carried out by the U.S. Treasury in a way similar to how the Treasury in conjuction with the Fed monetizes (finds the money for) the legislated "budgets" presented to them now, with the critical difference being that it would be monetized directly with currency that was issued out of the Treasury, instead of financed by funds raised through a convoluted process of taxation and "borrowing" via the sale of bonds.

I would hasten to assert that creating a monetization picture is not some sort of socialistic planning process. It is, rather, a setting up of monetary parameters that would enable the private economy to operate fully, without spinning out of control in a fit of "inflation", "deflation", "business contraction", or whatever. Money would be issued directly to fund the services that government agencies perform or pay for. As it is "spent" it goes into circulation, and thereby becomes available to the private economy as circulating medium.

The Federal government would no longer need to find a source of revenue because it is itself the source of money, and therefore could create and "spend" into circulation as much or as little as it needed to pay its bills. There would still be "taxation" on the Federal level, but their purpose would no longer be to pay for anything. The authority to monetize would take care of that. Rather, this device would be used to regulate the amount of money in circulation. It would act in the manner of an overflow device for the monetary pool. The rate of taxation, then, would be set according to the "depth of liquidity" (i.e. currency) that would maintain the pool at an optimal level. All monies collected through Federal taxation could be thought of as being extinguished, with a fresh supply to be recreated and issued for subsequent expenses as needed.

Understood this way, the subject of taxes would, I believe, cease to be the source of emotionalism and demogoguery in the public discourse. Taxing rates would be set higher or lower, not according to some ideological notion of whether we are paying "too much" or "too little", but as a calculated dependent variable in the monitization picture that would be adjusted to set the amount of money in circulation at a level that is proportional to the economic activity it is intended to facilitate. The process would be transparant and the resulting rates rendered evident to the extent that the public would likely find them to be only minimally arguable, if at all. It is likely that the fine tuning of the rate could be left to the Treasury Department, as the political questions would have already been addressed in the National Economic Picture, and the actual setting of the tax rate would become essentially a matter of course that is best handled administratively. These are details that can be worked out as long as the process is upfront and understandable to the public.

Imagine the harmony that could break out in the political discourse with the issue of taxes being essentially understood, not as a way for government to get its "greedy hands" on ones money, but as an integral part of a transparent monetization process that would insure to the people an adequate-supply of cost free money. This would be enhanced by the reality that if the Treasury issued the currency, the net transfer of dollars occssioned by the supposed "need" to pay investors "interest" on the "debt" backing the the money supply would be eliminated, thereby relieving the political pressure to use taxation to redistribute income back to the segment of the population who are net losers in the interest-payment game. I venture to predict that the willingness of the public to cooperate with the taxation regime would rise dramatically.

This monetization process is very much in the spirit of Ben Franklin, who, when asked how he could explain the prosperous condition of the Colonies despite the fact they were borrowing so little money from the banks, answered:

"That is simple. It is only because in the Colonies we issue our own money. It is called colonial scrip, and we issue it in proper proportion to the demand of trade and industry."

It is the actual productive capacity of the real economy that backs the money. This is true now, and has always been so. Why, then, cannot the people's economy be supplied with money issued directly out of the public agency constituted with the expressed constitutional power to do so? Bonds are merely fancy slips of paper. They produce nothing; therefore they underwrite nothing.

Why, then, have they been permitted to be interjected a presumed essential link in the monetization process? As it is now, the public Treasury effectively prints both the money and the bonds, hands the money over to the Fed, and then "borrows" it back in exchange for these gilded promises to pay "interest". The bizzare logic of this routine was challenged by Congressman Patman when he stated:

"The dollar represents a one dollar debt to the Federal Reserve System. The Federal Reserve Banks create money out of thin air to buy Government Bonds from the U.S. Treasury . . . and has created out of nothing a . . . debt which the American People are obliged to pay with interest."

"In many years of questioning high experts on the matter, I have yet to hear even one plausible answer to the question (of) why the Government should extend money-creating powers to the private commercial banks to be used, without cost, to create money which is lent to the Government at interest."

The power to monetize allows for the creation of an economic feedback loop between a society and its members. Monetization is, in a practical sense, how we as a nation impart to our social order equity and form. The ability to create its own circulating medium is an essential aspect of any society's sovereignty and self-actualization (which is why coins are often called "sovereigns"). The power to monetize is tantamount to the power of "self-government". It is an exercise, not only of "freedom" and "justice", but also of securing the essential "means to freedom and justice". The values of people on a cultural level can be said to be the initiator of a loop, which in turn affects how the National Economic Picture is constituted through the political process, out of which any economic surplus of the nation arises and is made available to be plowed back into the substantive ground of life (if it is not being skimmed off for "interest" charges), out of which the People, who initiate all culture, are nurtured. Thus is a threefold social spiral initiated at the cultural level, given a positive spin through the political life, and carried to fruition in the economic life, the surplus from which is then recycled back into the ground of the cultural life.

CHAPTER 5
VALUE-ADDED

The Concept of "Value-Added"

I have often asserted that the most fundamental "rule" of economics is that one should think first in images of the actual human and material realities of any economic situation, and only then add in the factor of money. As an exercise, let us track in our imagination the progress of a product as it emerges from the untapped resources of the earth, through its stages of production, and finally to its final use.

Before its extraction a natural element has no economic value, as it merely lies there in the ground. Presently someone comes along to mine it, pick it, hunt it, fish it, pump it, dig it, cut it down, doze it into a heap, or otherwise perform the task necessary to wrest it from the earth. When this raw material is gathered up into a form suitable to be offered in the marketplace, it has become a "commodity". Someone with a use for it in mind will then buy it as such. The tree has been drawn into the economic stream and made available for further use by the logger in that he has put work into transforming it from its natural standing disposition, to logs ready to be picked up at the landing for myriad uses. Economically speaking, the value of the logs represents a net increase of the value of the tree that can be described as "value-added".

It may happen that the party who shows up to haul away the logs wants them for personal firewood, the additional processing for which he will do himself. This buyer then becomes the "end user" or "consumer". In this case there was only one value-added increment between unrealized potential in the earth and end product.

More commonly, the person that shows up to purchase the logs does not want them for final consumption, but intends to process them into an intermediate product; a more refined commodity, if you will. He may, for example, be a lumberman looking to buy saw logs. He will pay a railroad to transport them to his mill, where he intends to saw them into lumber. From there a yard will buy the lumber, hire a trucker to transport it to their location, and place it on racks where it is more accessible to those who need lumber for their enterprise. Let us further suppose that a contractor buys the lumber and makes it into a house, which is then sold to a consumer who wants to live in it. If we track wood from earth-to-log-to-train-to-sawmill-to-truck-to-yard-to-contractor-to-consumer we can easily see that an increment of value has been added to the "tree" at each stage of the production process. In economic terms, each of these quantum increases is said to be the "net value-added" from a stage of production, and the sum of all these steps is the "total value-added" of the product.

Note that through this example so far, I have talked of value-added only in physical terms, with no direct reference to money. Ideally, money enters the picture as a medium of convenience to facilitate the exchanges necessary to facilitate the transformation and ultimate consumption of the product. Each worker who performs his task must be compensated according to his net "cost of production" (i.e. expenses incidental to performing his step in the process), plus receive a "profit" to cover his living expenses, plus have enough money left over to complete the next round of production. These value-added increments are typically expressed in monetary terms. It follows that these successive price increments (net value-added) accruing proportionally to each step in the process determines ultimately what a consumer would need to pay (total value-added) in order to maintain overall equity between producer and consumer. I call this process "value-added monetization".

"Monetizing" itself, then, is the way by which numerical value accrues to the physical value-added of a product as it works its way though the production process. In a narrow sense this figure is determined by the dynamics of equitable exchange in the marketplace. In a larger sense it is linked to the manner in which money enters into and is maintained within the market cycle.

To round out the above example, it should be noted that there is also an incidental cost of money that needs to be accounted for. Its value-added is determined by the actual work that is performed by people to bring currency in some form into being, make it convenient to the point of transaction, and facilitate the phases of its handling. These are real and necessary costs measured in material resources and human effort, and have to be covered as surely as the labors of the logger, trucker, millwright, lumber dealer and carpenter.

These real costs, however, should not be confused with the so-called "cost of money" expressed as "compounding interest" attached to a bank "loan". This "cost" is a misnomer. It is in actuality a fee that is affixed to the creation of money (for example, $100,000 mortgage) that only "pay back" an amount on the order of $300,000 for a 30–year contract. Of that total, $100,000 is accounted for as compensation for what was paid to the tradesmen who built the house, but $200,000 will go to the bank for the labor of writing a check and handling the subsequent paperwork. I would pose the question, for a house that costs $100,000 to build for actual construction work done, does it really "cost" $200,000 for the bank to process the paperwork? If we were generous and allow, say, $5,000 cover the bank's actual expenses for doing this task (which is performed for the most part automatically by computer these days), and a $5,000 (i.e. 100%) profit on that cost, that would bring the total that would have to be remitted by the buyer to $110,000. Keep in mind that there was virtually no expense related to bringing the $100,000 dollars into existence, since the principal amount of the "loan" was created by the mere writing of a check against no funds.

Other businesses bill for their work on a cost-plus-reasonable-profit basis. Why, then, is banking the only industry that can charge out their services on a compounding-interest-on-a-money-conjured-out-of-nothing basis? The answer is that it is the industry that has been accorded the privilege (or charged with the responsibility, depending on how one looks at it) of creating money out of thin air, and is the beneficiary of a monetary culture that is acquiesced to, albeit often reluctantly, by virtually everyone in the citizenry that deems this to be the right and natural way for them to do business. The charge is raised that this privileged is often "abused", and therefore needs to be "regulated"; abused or regulated as it may be, the result is still fundamentally the same.

I would hasten to add that the picture I have painted is somewhat simplistic. There are many factors at work here, which, if pursued, would explain why many banks are going broke anyway. Nevertheless, the anomaly created by this mortgage transaction is experienced as a burdensome reality, as anyone who has paid a mortgage can attest, and its effects ripple out through the entire social, political and economic life.

The Monetization Picture Expressed as "Value-Added"
The processing of this particular tree was, of course, not the only value-added economic activity going on in the economy in, say, a given year. There were millions of other trees and myriad

other resources being turned into a vast array of other products. What is more, particular raw commodities become combined, processed, transported, warehoused, and otherwise manipulated in a virtually infinitely complex weaving as they rise through the stages of the value-added production process. It is too big a task to create an accurate picture from this data if one is too caught up in the unworkable mass of details, but realistic estimates can be made and net increments calculated.

The problem is analogous to the effect of dumping a one-gallon bucket of water into the ocean. If we try to account for the effect of each molecule in the bucket of water as it interacts with each molecule in the ocean, we are quickly faced with a task so complex that one cannot even begin to make headway. After all, it is obvious that every molecule of water in that bucket must interact with every molecule in the ocean, and vise versa, for the ocean to find its new level. If we deal reasonably with net effects, however, the problem becomes very simple. If the volume of water in the bucket is divided by the surface area of the ocean, we can calculate in a minute on a hand-held scientific calculator the net rise in the ocean's level as a whole with perfect certainty and precision, however miniscule that increment may be.

The creation of a monetization picture is analogous to calculating the rise or fall of the economic ocean according to known increments of addition and subtraction, which can be measured as value-added. To predict its level from an analysis of its minute permutations for a body of economic liquidity as huge, complex, and dynamic as the national economy of the United States is humanly impossible, but if its constitution can be broken down into reasonable units of value-added, the problem becomes relatively simple. This can be done by making reasonable estimates of the value-added economic activity generated by various segments of the economy. From there, the level of currency needed to float the economic ship (the amount of money needed to be in circulation) can be estimated relatively accurately, and the results verified by tracking the aggregate rise or fall of prices over time.

This process is essentially what the Congress purports to do, and the public imagines this body to be doing now, but in reality that is not what is happening due to an analogous factor that has intervened and is not being properly accounted for; i.e. the ever-mounting loss of liquidity in the economy due to the charging of "interest" against the money supply. That is to say, real value-added additions to the economy do not have their expected effect, because the money that is created and added to the economy to represent them is constantly losing value due to the effect to the "interest" charges which are demanded as a condition for it even to exist.

Essentially, the bucket of money that is added to the economic ocean is a shrinking bucket, and the self-adjusting tendency of the ocean cannot achieve a stable level. The "investors" who have siphoned off this net shrinkage in the form of "interest" payments are as a rule willing, and even anxious, to release it back into the economic ocean, but only if someone approaches them to re-borrow with yet another "interest" charge that piggybacks on these dollars already burdened by the "interest" that attend their original issue. This sets up a compounding spiral in which the financial value of the original bucket tends toward disappearing altogether. It should not be surprising, then, that the benefit of the value-added of the economic enterprise that serves as collateral for the monetary pool is not financially realized. "Debt" multiplication co-opts value creation and the citizen, or, failing that, the government feels obliged to take on more "debt" to replace the liquidity ever-draining from the monetary pool.

If we truly "follow the money" (i.e. think through the consequences of the bank loan transaction), this sequence of cause and effect is itself transparent, but we have a monetary blind spot in our cultural consciousness that does not allow people for the most part to see it, not even bankers and Congressmen. Instead, we get caught up in analyzing the complexity of the micro movements and permutations of the water in the economic ocean. This, in turn, creates a froth of financial "thinking" that obscures transparency and results in what might be called "monetary denial".

"We must raise interest rates to dampen inflation", one pundit might cry. That is tantamount to dumping a one-gallon bucket of water into the economic ocean, and then expecting an undifferentiated one-gallon cylinder representing a reduced inflation rate to pop up somewhere else. A reduction in the rate of rise in prices may (or may not) manifest in the short run due to the dampening effect of the rate increase on the public's ability and willingness to move forward with economic confidence, but it is the resultant increasing "cost" of money that can only be covered by an increase in prices charged for goods and services as the "interest" payments become due over time that drives "inflation" in the long run. What is more, raising the "interest" affects all factors in the economic ocean, albeit some more that others.

Similarly another voice might urge, "We must restore fiscal balance by taking a bite out of the state budget." The laying-off of a certain number of people to meet that goal may indeed result in "restoring fiscal balance" – this year, but the resultant diminution of economic activity will of necessity have to be compensated for by all factors in the economic ocean. To think otherwise is to expect that the dipping of a bucket of water out of the ocean would show up as a neat, predictable bucket-shaped depression in the water (representing the "balancing of the budget") somewhere else. To start with, it will diminish the productive economic base that will be counted on to support next year's budget, and replace it with the need for greater welfare. People not working cannot produce, so how does it help the economy to lay off people from working, save to have a temporary effect on one isolated economic parameter (i.e. balancing this year's budget)?

The lesson here is that in monetary matters, everything that changes affects everything else, and it all must be accounted for in the economic ocean finding its own level. The individual and cultural denial on this wise has given rise to all manner of abstract theories, sectarian conflicts and ideological dogmatisms. These foster a culture of punditry that is forever pushing or pulling on this economic parameter, or that, expecting that it will have a neatly salutary result in some other factor.

As the arguments grow more vociferous or nuanced, these simple factors are multiplied and played against each other in ever-greater displays of financial sophistication. The result is essentially a churning of the intellectual waters whereby the transparency of the economic order is totally obscured. This can be remedied by returning to common sense, as applied to a straightforward observation of what is really happening when we "follow the money". The way to create a sound monetization picture, then, is to create pictures of real value-added economic activity projected in a reasonable way into the future out of the just-completed past, and then bring it to life with the injection of money that is not infected with the cancer of "debt".

One salutary effect of working with value-added analysis is that it tends to bring a revealing light to the question of what is really of value and what is not. For example, it is clear that ambulance services can be of lifesaving value, and who would suggest that there should not be an ample supply, or that they be denied to anyone in their moment of need? It begs to be asked, however, does a proliferation of ambulance rides across greater distances to emergency rooms already overwhelmed due to the effect of the closing of other emergency rooms caused by the chronic shortfall of funds available to maintain their existence due to the reliance of society on "debt"-based money really qualify as an economic activity of a value-adding sort? One might factor into this the possibility (arguably, probability, or even certainty) that the social diseases caused by "debt" sow the seeds for conditions that spawn an untoward level of need for ambulance rides in the first place. In any case, this expensive service has the financial effect of quickly inflating the nation's "Gross National Product" numbers, but in a human sense, are all ambulance rides equivalent to true value-added?

In our present economy, countless millions of human work hours are spent managing directly or indirectly the handling of "interest" charges on bank loans, but does that add value to our lives? I am not trying to make a value judgment of anyone's arena of livelihood. The fact is that we have virtually all found ourselves at some juncture feeling compelled to do what we had to do to survive, but an honest creation of a national economic picture based on valued-added would, in my view, create a positive discussion that would help us as individuals and collectively as a society to extricate ourselves from the morally and economically dubious enterprises in which we have increasingly found ourselves feeling obliged to engage. This cannot help but have a salutary effect on our elected representatives' legislative deliberations as well.

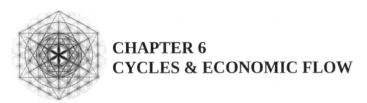

CHAPTER 6
CYCLES & ECONOMIC FLOW

Two Flows of Money – The Market Cycle and the Monetization Cycle

Money has <u>two flows</u>. The first is the "<u>market cycle</u>", which is the flow of money in the economy from the people who buy products ("consumers"), to the people that make them ("producers"), and then back again. Money spent by the consumer covers the costs to the producer of value-added work necessary to bring products into being. These funds are distributed as earned income to workers and profits to businessmen who performed that work, which they, in turn, take home in the form of paychecks or profit checks, which are spent by them as consumers for those products. And so the market cycle goes round-&-round in a continuous loop.

The second flow is the "<u>monetization cycle</u>". It is necessary that money flow not only through the closed loop of the market cycle, but also in and out of the loop itself. As a rule, the money supply in a market cycle must continually expand or contract in order to accommodate changing levels of economic activity. This breathing in and out of money with respect to the economy, therefore, is absolutely essential to match the fluctuating call for currency required to support prices that are stable with respect to value-added work.

This two-flows process is analogous to the workings of a hydraulic loop with a filtered fluid reservoir attached. We can liken the productive factor in the economy to the pump, and the needs of the consumer as the end use where its energy is expended. If there are no leaks in the system then every drop of fluid medium that leaves the pump will show up at the device that it drives, and in turn find its way back at the pump. This is true as a matter of principle. It is a closed system. If money is not allowed to leak into or out of the market cycle, it too forms a closed loop in which its flow will transfer energy in an equitable and predictable manner.

In addition, it is common with closed hydraulic loops that they need a way to expand and contract their fluid supply according to the demands of their work cycle, and this provides the opportunity to refresh the quality of the fluid (which is why it is often run through a filter). Likewise, the closed market cycle will need a way to expand and contract its money supply according to the level of economic activity it is called upon to serve, and this expansion and contraction provides the opportunity to refresh the quality of the money (by passing it through the filter of the legislated mandates).

The key to making any monetization scheme work equitably is to set it up so that the quantity of money in circulation is maintained in proportion to the fluctuating value-added enterprise it is meant to facilitate, and the money itself is periodically cleansed and re-injected (extinguished and reissued) in a socially optimal way.

Two Loops of the Monetization Cycle – Loan-&-Payback; Spending-&-Taxation

The monetization cycle itself has two loops. The <u>first loop</u> by which money can enter and exit the market cycle is a "<u>loan & payback</u>" mechanism. By this method money is injected into circulation through loans issued directly out of the Treasury. It should be noted that banks can act as agents in the field for such issuance with the stipulation that it is the U.S. Treasury that is authorizing the creation of monetary credits loaned, and receiving the proceeds of any interest or fees associated with the use of that money, beyond, that is, the actual costs to the bank itself of handling the paperwork. Equitable proportionality between an actual enterprise and the monetary injection that gives it life is maintained through socially enlightened discernment that guides the loan application process. Put more simply, the loan has to make sense.

Direct loans out of the Treasury could be made to any participant in the economy, private or public, but as a practical matter the total amount that could be loaned out would be limited by the need for money to come into circulation. Taken to its limit, it is theoretically possible that the nation's entire money supply could be loaned into circulation through this process. This is, in fact, what is done at present, except that under current practice the money so "borrowed" comes from the private banking system with an "interest" charge attached. Money from the public sector does not have to be loaned at interest (we as a society don't need to pay interest to ourselves). Alternately, if an interest charge were assessed, the proceeds would be remitted to the U.S. Treasury where they would be used to defray taxes. Once the monetary pool was filled, other would-be borrowers would have to borrow money already in circulation, as is done now through credit unions, savings-&-loans, and other forms of "banks of deposit" (banks that do not issue money, but instead "invests" the money of its depositors).

Besides needing to stay within the quantity required to fill the monetary pool, another major factor that would govern borrowing from the public sector relates to who would be deemed eligible for such funds, and for what purposes. That would be decided by the social will as expressed through legislated policy guidelines. One could imagine that such regulations would favor initiatives that were most essential to the common good.

A likely candidate for such treatment would be loans to state and local governmental bodies for needed infrastructure improvements. I have in fact been active in an effort to introduce such a proposal to the Congress via an initiative (the Concord Resolution) proposed to the Concord, Massachusetts town meeting. Communities commonly pay two or three times the cost of public works projects due to the interest charges associated with having to resort to the bond market for financing. As a consequence, needed work is often put off, skimped on, or not done at all. The failure of the levies in New Orleans and the collapsed bridge in Minneapolis are almost surely part of the cost, even above interest charges, that the nation has had to pay for such financially induced neglect.

Loans could also be made to private individuals as a matter of public policy, as in, for example, making them available for low-income housing.

In the course of talking to people about the Concord Resolution, I have often heard the concern expressed that the privilege of borrowing interest-free money directly from the public domain would be tantamount to offering "free money", or at least "cheap money", and so would lead to abuse. I understand their concern, but I would answer that it could not be construed as "free money", because it would need to be paid back. If it were decided that the "market discipline" of charging interest were required to assure that people took these loans seriously, then an interest charge could indeed be assessed, the proceeds from which would then be used by the Treasury to defray taxes. Presumably, as in any loaning process (ideally), competent people would oversee the process, and measures to insure accountability would be in place.

At the core of discipline-of-the-market argument put forth by folks who distrust what would happen if the Treasury loaned out interest-free money, even to responsible public bodies, is the question, "What would keep this process from becoming a feeding frenzy at the public trough?" I would answer first of all that the very premise on which the present privately-based system is founded is "something-for-nothing". That is, it is presumed in the current financial culture that money created out thin air from the awarding of a public franchise to a privileged segment of the economy can "earn" more money, without the expenditure of further productive effort on the part of those who hold the contracts against the money so introduced into circulation. This is, in my view, the very essence of something-for-nothing institutionalized. The apotheosis of this belief has left a great train of damage and suffering in its wake, and there is no hope that I can see for the system redeeming itself in the long run while the money-for-nothing secular religion holds sway in people's hearts and minds. Indeed, is not the current monetary crisis a telling sign of the collective irresponsibility that we as a nation have fallen into by allowing the money-for-nothing gambit that is at the heart of the creating-money-privately-out-of-thin-air-and-expecting-to-receive-an-endlessly-compounding-"return" principle free reign, until it is now running amok? Why is it that we as a democratic society can trust ourselves to have children, raise families, establish communities, run businesses, alter the earth with a vast infrastructure, go to the moon, tamper with the genome, establish our own laws, run our own courts, elect our own leaders, and act out life-or-death decisions in countless ways, including going to war, but feel compelled to abdicate the control over our own monetary powers to unaccountable others because we don't trust that *We the People* can handle it?

There is discernment in realism, but no power in cynicism. The issue of money creation, I believe, calls us as individuals and as a society to face where, as the better part of wisdom, we would draw the line between the two. I for one do not see how we can call ourselves responsible as individuals or as a society if we do not take control of our own monetary franchise. Our failure to do so has wreaked havoc, both within the nation, and now throughout the world. That there is potential for abuse is clear enough, but if we as a democratic nation are resolved that "... *government of the people, by the people, for the people, shall not perish from the earth*", it seriously behooves us to face everything and avoid nothing. Money, I would suggest, is the core issue that calls us to account on that hope. The "everything" that needs to be faced, and dare not be avoided, surely includes taking dominion over the creation, issuance and control over our own coin of the realm. We have no chance, I would suggest, to exercise ultimate responsibility in any domain of our lives until we do.

The <u>second loop</u> by which money can enter and exit the market cycle is "<u>direct monetization</u>" by the Federal government. This would tend to have the appearance of government "spending" as conceived of at present, but "spending" is not an accurate expression in this case. The word implies the drawing down of a limited pool of money, which in turn must be replenished. "Monetization", in contrast, proceeds out of the social franchise to create money in whatever abundance is needed. It is, properly speaking, a fiat of the social will expressed through the political process. There is no limit to this reservoir of created funds, and so government, as the monetizing agency, does not have to find the money to "spend", only the will and wit to monetize wisely.

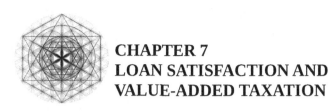

CHAPTER 7
LOAN SATISFACTION AND
VALUE-ADDED TAXATION

Loan Satisfaction and Value-Added Taxation

If there is a continuous pouring of money into the economic stream via the monetization process, then there must be means to take the excess back out. This is necessary for several reasons. The process of retiring excess currency provides the opportunity to inject new funds in the next fiscal cycle. Fresh flows can be directed to water, so to speak, a socially optimal economic base that is focused on basic human needs. This is necessary to maintain a social welfare base in the economy. It keeps alive the perpetual opportunity for new enterprise and the generation of value-added in service to people's immediate needs and humanity's evolutionary aspirations. Finally, the retirement of currency keeps it from getting "old"; i.e. stagnant in unproductive corners. Currency retirement through taxation provides the opportunity for the social order to maintain control of its monetization process. If money is merely put out there and left to perpetually circulate subject to a "market forces", that is effectively an invitation for those with less than altruistic intent to progressively co-opt the process. It would tend to lead, I suggest, to the result intended in the *Monopoly* board game referred to above.

I realize that these thoughts are stated very broadly, but I don't have the space to do them justice in this treatise. They are the cutting edge of important principles that affect the economic order. It is my intent to expand the discussion to a more comprehensive level into the future.

This raises the question – "What are the mechanisms in practice by which the retirement of money can be expeditiously and equitably accomplished?" Basically there are two, and they correspond respectively to the dual loops of monetization cycle.

The quantity of money put into circulation via the "<u>loan & payback</u>" mode is self-regulated by payback of the loans. That is simple enough.

The quantity of money put into circulation via the "<u>direct monetization</u>" mode is regulated by "<u>taxation</u>". In practice this is more problematic. I would reiterate here in the most emphatic terms – <u>With respect to the activities of the Federal government, taxes do</u>

<u>not pay for anything. The power to monetize does that</u>. The Feds do not have to find money to do business. They hold the monetization franchise. That is to say, they have in their grasp a checking account with infinite reserves. Under such a circumstance, taxes in reality serve as an overflow device for the pool of money poured into the economy by direct monetization. In addition, if some loans fail, the reclamation of those monies is also rolled over into the taxation mechanism.

The pertinent question becomes, then, what manner of taxation would be most expeditious to employ? Before giving a specific answer to that question, I would bring the reader's attention to a pattern that is exhibited in the above enumeration of the principle of value-added and how that relates to the monetization picture. As value accrues to a product as it rises through the production hierarchy towards its ultimate destiny as a final product, it does so in increments which are expressed as value-added. Furthermore, money enters the picture as an increasing price of the product in the making as it passes from hand-of-tradesman to hand-of-tradesman through stages of the production process, and does so in equitable proportion to the value-added at each increment. The establishment of this step-by-step proportional relationship depends on there being a proper amount of money in circulation and a spirit of equity in all transactions. The maintenance of this principle is the key to making money the servant of real-life economic activity, instead of having life serve money. I reiterate this because the key to effective and equitable taxation is to implement it in such a way that it is in harmony with the value-added monetization process. In principle, then, it would be the better part of wisdom, in my view, that taxation be applied proportionally to the value-added increments of economic activity.

This is nothing new. The European and Canadian taxing regimes are already based upon value-added. Fundamentally, there are two forms which "<u>value-added taxation</u>" can take on. One is to apply it as an income tax at a flat rate. This is the so-called "<u>flat tax</u>" that was much talked about (though not in a fully conscious way) in the American political scene in the '90's (introduced primarily by Jerry Brown in his Presidential campaign). The virtue of the scheme is that if the rate is assessed uniformly to all income, it is tantamount to applying it to all value-added. In order to remain truly "flat", the tax must be applied at a single percentage rate across the entire spectrum of value-added activity. This rate would calculated on the basis of what is required to retire the sum of money that comes into circulation through direct monetization, plus roll-overs from defaulted loans, plus increases or minus decreases in the money supply. As such the flat-tax, properly applied, is an integral feature of the direct monetization principle. As such, it may be called a "value-added monetization factor".

The second possible mode of value-added taxation is the "<u>sales tax</u>". This is assessed at the point of sale of the final product. People are familiar with a form of the sales tax as applied at retail outlets. It is value-added in concept because the final price of any item is by definition the sum of value-added increments that were inherent in its bringing it to market. There are technical problems associated with determining when each item in the production chain has reached its final stage of consumption, but that, I am sure, is a devil-in-the-details that can be worked out.

Relationship Between Loan Satisfaction and Value-Added Taxation

The basic challenge of the loan satisfaction process is to apply sufficient discretion such that the loans are actually able to be retired out of the proceeds of the enterprises for which they were issued. Within a non-usury monetization process, this is necessary, not to keep the system from going "bankrupt" (that can't happen), but to assure an equitable orderliness to the process. In real life there can arise situations where loan repayment is delayed excessively, or never consummated at all. This can happen for reasons of default, but in the absence of a net "cost-of-money" burden that would need to be borne by participants, public and private, in the economy, we can expect that the rate of default on loans made out of the Treasury would be low. It may also come to pass that some loans would be forgiven for humanitarian considerations or overarching social priorities. Whatever the reasons for non-payment, a question arises as to how "non-performing loans" (to invoke the banking term for the phenomenon) would be covered in the monetizing scheme.

Just as any benefits from interest charges would accrue to the Treasury and be used to defray taxes, so would any shortfall in loan repayments be recovered by taxation. It should be noted that this is still not a net loss to the country as a whole. Monies that were borrowed and never repaid would remain in circulation as if they had been simply "spent" into circulation through direct monetization. It would be natural, then, for them to be regulated by the same taxation mechanism that is used to control the amount of money that is maintained in circulation via direct monetization.

The nation could elect to adopt a monetization policy by which the entire money supply essentially was issued into circulation as the principal proceeds of loans out of the U.S. Treasury. This is precisely how the money supply is maintained now, except that the loans are from private banks.

It is also possible that the amount of money introduced into circulation via the loaning mechanism could exceed the amount that is needed to maintain the market cycle at a stable (i.e. "non-inflationary") price level. This is also precisely what happens now, which is why most of the money issued by the Fed is actually kept out of circulation through the sale of bonds (which accounts for the $12 trillion-plus that is represented as "Federal debt"). Within a public monetary regime, funds introduced into circulation via the loaning mechanism that are in excess to what is needed to fill the monetary pool could be drawn out and withheld from circulation via taxation, instead of bonds. This would obviate the supposed need to pay "interest" on the funds so held in abeyance. These monies would then be available to be released back into the money supply as needed, where they would become available in due time to repay the Treasury for it loans.

There is a balance that would need to be set as matter of public policy as to how much of the money supply is to enter via loans vs direct monetization ("spending"). At one extreme, as noted above, the entire money supply could be issued as loans, and taxation limited to what is required to take the money out of circulation that was issued for loans that defaulted or were forgiven. At the other end of the spectrum, the entire money supply could be spent directly into circulation, and taxation would then be used in a very straightforward way to maintain the amount of money so issued at an optimum level in the circulating currency pool. In reality, it is likely that some combination of the two modes would be utilized.

The amount of the money supply that is "spent" into circulation is directly dependent upon the portion of the national economy that those funds are intended to activate. For example, let us suppose that the total value-added of economic activity in the nation in a given year is expected to be financially equivalent to $10 trillion dollars. For the sake of simplicity, let us suppose also that the only method used to inject money into the money supply is direct monetization (i.e. loans out of the Treasury are not made). Let us suppose further that the amount of economic activity that the Federal government would be legislated to perform or finance in that year amounted to $1.5 trillion. This is akin to a yearly "budget" of $1.5 trillion as it is commonly thought of at present. Accordingly, $1.5 trillion dollars would be created by the Treasury and "spent" into circulation to cover the expenses of the government for that year. This $1.5 trillion would represent 15 percent of the economic activity that would take place in the economy for that year.

If this $1.5 trillion dollars were injected into the economy and left to circulate, it would soon increase the amount of money in circulation to the point where prices would begin to rise, causing what in present parlance is described as "inflation". If we were to assume that the economy was operating at a stable level of economic activity, such that it would be desirable to maintain the amount of money in circulation at a constant level from one year to the next, then that $1.5 trillion dollars injected over a year through Federal monetization would have to be taken back out over the same year. This could be accomplished by levying a 15 percent tax against all value-added economic activity in the form of a 15 percent flat tax against income or a 15 percent sales tax.

If it were deemed desirable to increase the amount of money in circulation, the taxing rate would be adjusted to a percentage that was lower than the percentage of the GNVA (Gross National Value-Added) that Federal monetization was expected to finance. For example, if the GNVA was $10 trillion, and of that total the Federal government was expected to monetize its portion with the issuance of $1.5 trillion, or 15 percent of the total, and it was further decided that money supply over a given year would need to be increased by $100 million (one percent of the GNVA), this could be accomplished by lowering the taxation rate over a year by one percent; from ten percent to nine percent. A similar determination would then be made for the next year as to whether this differential between the rate of taxation and the percent of the GNVA the Federal government would monetize would be carried forward, thereby continuing the net pouring of additional money into the money supply, or alternately, the taxation rate would be returned to matching the percent of the GNVA that the Federal government was meant to monetize, thereby stabilizing the money supply at its present level.

Conversely, the money supply could be adjusted downward in a given year by increasing the rate of taxation to a level that exceeds the percentage of the GNVA the Federal government is assigned to monetize, and the question of whether or not to continue that policy would be determined in the following year.

The Trade Turn

The next question that naturally arises is, "At what level should the money supply be maintained?" To answer that question, it needs to be noted that each dollar in circulation, on average, will change hands a certain number of times in a year, which number could be described as the "trade turn" (or in more orthodox economic terms, the "multiplier" or "velocity of money").

Let us suppose that the "trade turn" in a given point in time is "ten". That means that a dollar circulating in the economy would on average change hands in the purchase of goods and services ten times in a year. If it were anticipated that the participants in the economy would tend to do $10 trillion worth of value-added economic activity (GVNA = $10 trillion), then that would require a circulating money supply of one trillion ($1 trillion x 10 = $10 trillion). If dollars tended to change hands at half that rate (trade turn = 5), then twice as many dollars would be needed to be in circulation to achieve the same result ($2 trillion x 5 = $10 trillion). Conversely, if dollars changed hands at twice that rate (trade turn = 20), then half as many dollars would be needed in the monetary pool ($0.5 trillion x 20 - $10 trillion).

One point of note here is that, in a macro (national) monetary sense, it would be just as easy to issue a high or low amount of money to achieve a certain level of economic GNVA, according to a known number for the trade turn. In the end, the trade turn and the money supply are parameters that bear a mathematically inverse relationship to each other.

The next question would be, "How is the trade turn determined?" The answer is that it is simply arrived at through statistical observation. It doesn't govern people, but allows them to live their economic lives freely, while facilitating the maintenance of an optimum amount of money in circulation to facilitate that.

The trade turn is a measure of the cultural, technological and financial factors at work in how people use money. For example, if people were frugal in their habits the trade turn would be relatively low (i.e. money would change hands slowly). Conversely, it would be relatively high if people were more profligate in their habits.

A greater employment of technology tends to increase the trade turn, as it generally creates a greater need for financial resources to accomplish the same task. For example, an intensely-mechanized, high-tech, non-local mode of agriculture tends to increase the amount of money required to put an ear of corn on the family table, and this is reflected in quicker capital flows. On the other hand, a more organic, low-tech, localized form of agriculture tends to need greatly reduced flows of capital to produce the same product (there is in fact a "slow money" movement that advocates precisely such an ethic).

The use of electronic means to move money tends to increase the frequency of its use, while the reliance on good old fashioned cash or personal checks tends to slow it down.

These are just a few factors that affect the trade turn, and the public dialogue by which the number associated with the actual rate is recognized could help to make us as a citizenry more conscious of how we use money, and the finer aspects of our relationship to it. This, in turn, would tend to insure that the monetization process is rendered transparent.

Some Additional Thoughts on Taxation

The basic challenge of a flat-tax regime is to collect the tax without impinging on the private affairs and personal freedom of the taxpayer. The process entails a reporting of one's personal income. For a person not in business, this would basically be a number. For those that would bundle their economic existence into a household, this would mean a bundling of each person's number. For those engaged in production it would mean the reporting of the net difference between costs-of-production and price-at-point-of-sale that is the economic determiner of value-added.

A flat tax does not inherently require the reporting of personal data beyond identifying oneself. If people can typically comprehend the general structure of the monetization regime, and can see its inherent equity, then it may not be too much to assume that any minimum requirement to make it work would be met with a willingness to comply. The taxation process can be done essentially as a routine bookkeeping procedure, with minimum intrusion into the managing of personal finances or doing business. The advantage of the flat-tax (as opposed to sales tax) is that it lends itself to a comprehensive coverage of all monetary manifestations of value-added as a matter of course, without gaps or overlap. A practical rub enters in that some sort of interface is required to give oneself an identity within the system. This may be in the form of a tax ID, social security number, or perhaps one's name rendered with unique specificity, or the name of one's enterprise. It can be argued that such a point of contact is a minimum requirement of a just and orderly social regime in any case.

On the face of it the sales tax is less intrusive because it can be paid anonymously, but it has its own complications. There is an issue of equity in that the burden of collecting and remitting taxes falls unevenly upon those who are in the retail business. A further complication arises in that the final use of some products is actually a cost for some production process. For example, virtually any hardware store sells its wares both to final consumers, and to tradesmen for whom the items represent not consumption, but a production cost. If these production items are not separated out, the value added represented by those items will be covered redundantly in the final purchase price for those items. There is a fair amount of paperwork required to keep this all sorted out, and this is intrusive in itself. The division of usage in real terms tends to become muddled in any case, so consequently gaps and overlaps will tend to arise in the coverage of the value-added base.

A variation of the sales tax idea that might clear up most of its inherent problems is to charge the tax, not on the final price of the item, but on the markup applied by the seller. Through the stages of any production process this would applied to the net value-added realized by that step in the process, as determined by subtracting the cost of production from price at sale (whether the customer is the end-user or the next participant in the production chain).

In the final analysis, for matters of taxation the devil is in the details. The ultimate challenge is to collect taxes in such a way that compliance is completely voluntary. To be sure, taxation in the current mindset is firmly linked with the idea of compulsion, but it cannot remain that way if we are ever to have a truly free society. They key to making that happen is to establish the whole monetization scheme on an equitable principle that is transparent to everyone, and to formulate whatever taxing mode is utilized as an integral part of that system. People will comply with something they can see and resonate with.

This proposition will, predictably, be met with the assertion that voluntary compliance will never work due to the untrustworthiness of human nature, but I would question that. We human beings have virtually all grown up in a system that has been a horror of inequity. What would people be like if they were nurtured in a culture that was morally consistent? Does anybody know? Why should we assume the worst? The monetizing and taxing system we have now is a monster of provocation, intrusion and dis-economy, yet out of their own good nature people tend to exhibit a high degree of willing compliance even now. I would invite anyone to stand by most any retail counter and witness it in human reality. There is a great deal of generosity and warmth exhibited in the course of even those most ordinary of exchanges. We tend to forget the witness that could be had from what is routinely right before our eyes.

The Question of "Government"

The hyper-loaded term "government" has been introduced here, and so must be dealt with lest it short circuit the discussion. To be sure, a "political life" to administer common affairs must arise, but this should be understood in terms of what people working in concert with each other for the sake of the commonweal do (Lincoln's proverbial "government of, by and for the People"), as opposed to a soulless specter that stands over the populace and controls it for spurious ends. An association of people working together to perform the social functions necessary to the commonweal is by definition a "government", but it is well to have a picture to associate with that word so that it does not poison the discussion.

For a perspective on this matter one could ask an old-time farmer what a "governor" is. He will point to two brass balls attached to a lever mechanism whirling about at the top of his steam tractor (newer machines have less-visible equivalents). This is a device that is connected to the throttle, which in turn governs the supply of air/fuel mixture admitted to the engine. The whole linkage is designed such that it expedites the running of the tractor in a continuous manner up to its full potential, but protects it from revving out of control. The settings of the governor can, of course, be changed to fine tune the performance of the equipment, but it does not assume any other level of control. It does not drive the tractor where it would go; the farmer continues to do that.

When I use the term "government" in relation to the monetization process, it is in a similar sense. Money is the air/fuel (spiritual/material) mixture that the economic engine runs on. Its flow needs to be governed in a way that is transparent to the social body it serves (the governors on steam tractors were always out in the open where one could plainly witness their operation), but should not be used as an instrument of meddling or control by partial interests (governors on steam tractors were limited in their control over the machine by the impartial laws of physics). Thus government (as for governors on steam tractors) are both enablers and limiters for the arrangements they govern.

Governments, as human institutions, are vastly more complex that governors on tractors, of course, but still I think that there is a principle demonstrated by the analogy that can be applied to government in a natural way that is not burdened with ideology. The setting up of a National Economic Picture is the natural mechanism for the optimal "governing" (both unleashing the production and setting the limits) of the economic engine by which the social order harnesses the productive power of its enterprising nature.

This rumination does not purport to be any final answer to the national economic conundrum. It is merely a rationalization of the conditions as they exist right now, and as such constitute a prospective starting point for a new economic evolution into the future. In the course of such I would anticipate that the nation's, and, in turn, humankind's economic activities will take on a character such that they become progressively more elegant and symbiotic with the natural order. The resultant transformation will be effectively a going back to the Garden. Within such a context, considerations traditionally associated with money, including monetization and taxation, will take on a new form and meaning. The devil hiding in the details might just flee if it were obliged to work in the Light.

CHAPTER 8
INTRODUCTION TO GEM

International Currency Normalization

At Bretton Woods, New Hampshire in 1944, the U.S. dollar was designated officially as the "reserve currency" ("paper gold") for every other macro-currency in the world. Technically, this agreement has lapsed since President Nixon ended the redemption of dollars in gold for foreign nationals in 1971, but by then the structural preeminence of the dollar was so entrenched that it was deemed practically impossible (save by immense disruption) to change its reserve status. The structural problems caused by the "debt"-based nature of the dollar, however, could be changed on a national level, thereby taking the world off the "debt" standard as well. This singular measure would plant the seed for a worldwide rectification of the global economic order. How, then, might this transformation be managed?

Almost anyone who has taken a year of high school algebra has been introduced to the concept that the relationship between "n" variables can be resolved if one can set them up in "n" simultaneous equations. The simplest case of two variables in two equations may look familiar:

$$a_1 x + b_1 y = c_1$$
$$a_2 x + b_2 y = c_2$$

Any algebra text will outline a solution which involves arranging the constants a_1, a_2, b_1, b_2, c_1 and c_2 in arrays called determinants, which are then expanded by simple arithmetic operations to render specific values for x and y respectively. This idea can be expanded to any number of variables in a corresponding number of equations. This in a nutshell is the key to the solution of the global trade dilemma.

There exist in the world at present some 180 macro currencies. Ideally the relationship between them could be set up as 180 equations with 180 variables. These could then be resolved by setting them up in arrays, which would be expanded in an algorithm which was identical to that used for the smaller dimensioned problems taught in high school. While the handling of the numbers would get a bit bulky, the calculation would present no challenge whatsoever to a computer.

The expansion would render a unique solution for each variable; i.e. each currency. This number would not be a measure of value in any absolute sense, but rather a factor that was relative to the solutions for all other variables. A comparison between any two factors would give a working ratio between their relative values in the context of a world trading system that was in equilibrium.

The virtues of the simultaneous-equation solution are manifold. Not the least of these is that the arrangement is freely "associative". That is, it describes a matrix of relationships that pulses and floats with no fixed point or baseline of reference above the life-economic, as determined by transactions that are freely entered into. The trading aggregates that the currency variables represent are determined in value-for-value exchanges between people, the values of which are expressed as "price". Moreover, it is in this value-for-value nexus that all factors of the life-economic, those calculable and those not, find their ultimate expression.

Another virtue of the scheme is its "transparency". Trading aggregates could be published, perhaps even in-progress in real time. We can be confident that there would be computer-savvy folk out there who would track this process, and make sure that the outcomes are what they are purported to be. Such feedback looping would also entail an ongoing dialogue on the life-economic values the parameters inculcate. Even if one were not personally able or inclined to do the math, the broad outlines of the procedure are still understandable and visible. It would be extremely difficult to hide anything from the body public, or get off track in a major way.

Much like for the turning from avarice in the cultural (micro) economic dimension, or elimination of "debt"-based currency in the national (macro), this solution is so self-evident that it is inexplicable that the world has not yet seized upon the concept (though I suspect that similar calculations must be performed behind the scenes by financial institutions in their attempts to make sense of global trading). In a public discourse where one hears expressed a great deal of longing for structural balance, stability and fairness in world trade, currency normalization represents its direct expression rendered mathematically. There is no ideology in it. Rather, it is how a competent engineer would straightaway solve the problem if he were presented simply with its parameters. Why, then, don't we as a civilization see it? What stands in the way of its implementation? The answer in an outward sense may be approached in a systematic manner as laid out below.

The Global Economic Matrix (GEM)

For purposes of this discussion, permit me to give the solution for international currency normalization a name: i.e. the "Global Economic Matrix" (GEM). This moniker is consistent with and descriptive of its nature and function. To illustrate its workings in more detail let us assume a world in which there were 4 significant currencies. This would necessitate the setting up of a GEM consisting of four simultaneous equations in four variables:

$b_1x + c_1y + d_1z = a_1w$ which is the trade equation re: currency *"w"*
$a_2w + c_2y + c_2z = b_2x$ which is the trade equation re: currency *"x"*
$a_3w + b_3x + d_3z = c_3y$ which is the trade equation re: currency *"y"*
$a_4w + b_4x + c_4y = d_4z$ which is the trade equation re: currency *"z"*

Each equation is based on the assumption that the aggregate value of a currency which is passed to trading partners outside of its domestic market of origin within any given time period, is balanced inherently by the aggregate value of the currencies that enter. This is justified because when all the factors are boiled down, all trade is essentially stuff-for-stuff (otherwise how would it be trade). Naturally, there are many nuances to this idea that could be explored, and no doubt numerous questions that would be raised. I think, though, that the principle is sound, and any perturbations that might arise are inherently compensated for in the matrix, much in the manner of water finding its own level.

This set of equations can be rewritten as:
$a_1w + b_1x + c_1y - d_1z = 0$
$a_2w + b_2x - c_2y + d_2z = 0$
$a_3w - b_3x + c_3y + c_3z = 0$
$-a_4w + b_4x + c_4y + d_4z = 0$

The next step is to plug in values for $a_1, a_2, a_3, a_4, b_1, b_2 \ldots d_4$, which represent the actual units of each respective currency that pass from one economy to another in the course of trading in goods and services (as per "balance of trade" as commonly perceived), and resolve the equations for each variable. Since this determinant is a special form where each of the equations add up to zero, there will not be a solution in which any variable can be expressed as a definitive numerical value. Rather, it will produce results that are unique in the sense that each variable can be resolved as a given ratio to any other variable, but not as a specific number.

The next step is to assign a value constant to one of the currencies (most likely a "1"). That then becomes the currency of reference, and all others could then be expressed as a specific numerical factor. A comparison of any two factors would produce a true ratio of values between currencies that would be consistent with world trade that is structurally balanced (i.e. normalized) as a whole.

It should be noted that numbers are rendered by this algorithm are not units of measure. Moreover, it would not be proper to say that they constitute a global currency, whether individually (as say the reference currency), or as a solution set. Such imprecise language would be a misrepresentation of the nature of the GEM. Accordingly, any resolution of the array associated with a given variable should be termed a "factor" to avoid slipping into a linguistic limbo. For purposes of this discussion, I will dub the solution to the matrix as the set of "Relative Currency Factors" (RCF's), with the numerical ratio associated with a given currency, when compared with a reference currency, being its respective "RCF".

Theoretically the expansion of the matrix (i.e. calculations of the RCF's) could be done at any interval, perhaps even continually in "real time", but I suggest that it would make sense to do it annually, given that the predominant life processes, of which money is an emanation, generally have a yearly basis related to the seasons, agriculture, holidays and festivals, fiscal years, etc. As a practical matter, it takes a full-year cycle to determine approximately what any currency is practically worth.

This would mean that the actual relative trading values of the world's currencies would, from one year to the next, tend to drift a bit off the mark. There is no way to avoid this since living factors in the economic life are always in motion. Assuming that trading patterns would settle into relatively stable relationships, this would be a limited problem, as the trading matrix would undergo a re-normalization the next year as a matter of course.

If one currency were designated as having an RCF of "1", then the RCF of any currency with respect to that reference currency could be expressed as a single positive number that could, in turn, be compared to any other in a one-step mathematical calculation.

To illustrate how this would all work, let us imagine that in our four-currency world we assigned to currency "w" the value of "1", and that the ratio between that currency and "x", "y" and "z" turned out to be 1.5, 8.7 and 0.24, respectively. That means that to find the relative trading worth of a unit of currency "x" compared to a unit of currency "z", one would simply divide the RCF of "x" by the RCF of "z" to arrive a "Trading Ratio" (TR) of 6.25 (1.5 ÷ 0.24 = 6.25). In other words, it would take 6.25 units of currency "x" to have the same nominal purchasing power of a unit of "z". By a similar calculation one could arrive at the nominal relative worth of one currency to any other in the matrix regardless of how many currencies that came to be.

The Global Trading Registry (GTR)

To make this scheme work in practice, there would need to be established a "Global Trade Registry" (GTR). It would function as an account clearing house which would tally units of currency that cross political boundaries in the course of trade between sovereign economic entities (i.e., those nations or economic unions [groups of nations] that choose to express sovereignty by issuing a currency), much as any "balance of trade" reckoning is performed at present. To be clear, this crossing of boundaries is not limited to the geographical periphery of the economic entity that issued the currency. For example, a British pound that passed from Brazil to Argentina in the course of commerce would be duly registered as passing from Brazil to Argentina, and show up therefore in the currency equations of Brazil and Argentina (but not Britain, as this pound would not represent a net transfer of currency into or out of Britain).

The method by which currencies could be tracked is simple and straightforward. An inventory would be taken on the prescribed fiscal date (suggest calling it the "jubilee") of the amount of each currency on deposit in each bank in every country for which there is a CRF represented in the GEM. These figures would be tallied to find the sum of each currency that actually resides within each respective political jurisdiction. The difference between this and last year's totals for a given currency within a specific political boundary would be the measure of its net movement into or out of that political entity. This number would then be entered as the constant associated with that currency in the trade equation for that political entity. The trade equations of all the political entities would be combined (essentially stacked one above the other) to form a mathematical matrix that that would then be expanded by a simple formula to arrive at a numerical value for each currency variable (RCF) that would be normalized to every other currency variable.

The GEM – Its Associative Nature

The most fundamental virtue of the GEM is its "associative" nature. That is to say, it is generated from the free association of economic entities in value-for-value trading, and has no fixed point or baseline of reference. It pulses and floats over the interplay of cultural (micro) and national (macro) economic intercourse in a transcendent manner that faithfully mirrors the economic life as a whole. It is eminently determinable, and yet moves with and accounts for virtually every economic variation in life, from the minute to the all-encompassing. The variables within the array are expressions of the net trading worth of each macro-economy, which in turn are true aggregates of the micro-enterprise activity within them.

The associative principle upon which the GEM is constructed could be likened to one that has long been recognized by science in situations where net effects and equilibriums are relevant, but the factors from which they arise are unworkably minute, complex and chaotic. This idea was summarized succinctly by French mathematician Jules Henri Poincare, who, when speaking of the difficulty of determining the pressure exerted by a confined gas from calculating the path of each molecule, stated :

"If by ill-luck I happen to know the laws which govern them I should be helpless. I should be lost in calculations and could never supply you with an answer to your questions. Fortunately for both of us, I am completely ignorant about the matter. I can therefore supply you with an answer at once. That may seem odd; but there is something odder still, namely that my answer will be right".

The problem of calculating anything in the life-economic is much like this, but with an additional complicating factor. We are talking about a phenomenon that is not only physically complex, but the variables thereof are human, with all the capriciously indeterminable vagary that implies. Nevertheless, using the GEM we can perform precise calculations and arrive at sure determinations about the net factors of the whole of the economic life, from the major to the minute.

One point of note is that within the context of this process political boundaries would effectively function, not as demarcations of inequity, armored frontiers, or coercive lines control, but rather as socially determined detection devises that can serve to assure that those who engage in commerce can carry on in full confidence that it will transpire within a matrix of relationships which trends organically towards a just and equitable pricing structure. This is the Holy Grail of "level playing field" much talked about, but little understood, by the sincere proponents of "free trade".

Notwithstanding, the GEM idea is sure to raise many questions as to what would happen in this or that particular situation. Could it accommodate the changes, perturbations and human variables that are sure to arise? I think such concerns are answerable if we think the GEM principle through to the end.

The GEM - An Ocean Analogy

By way of analogy, the principle at work in the GEM could be compared to the proposition of determining the effects of pouring a liter-cylinder of water into the ocean. While the nature of the molecular interactions affecting the case are largely known, any attempt to calculate results based on tracking them would be futile due to the virtually infinite complexity of the interactions that would take place. We can be sure, nonetheless, that every molecule in the ocean will have to accommodate and adjust its relationships to all other molecules with respect to the tiny body of water contained in that liter, and vise versa. What is most astonishing is that the net change in ocean level could be readily calculated with great precision. While it is true that vast quantities of water are leaving and entering the ocean at any given instant, and that it is subject to powerful undercurrents and surface disturbances, we can be certain that the net affect from that single liter of water is still real, abiding and calculable.

In principle the GEM behaves much like this. A minuscule change in any macro-currency, which in turn is subject to subtle changes in the micro-activity of which each is the aggregate, would be faithfully reflected in the whole (howbeit in the n'th decimal place). Moreover, these material and life factors that affect the array are in part knowable, but for all practical purposes as incalculable as the darting of water molecules in the ocean. This is true for reasons of imponderable complexity, but also due to the whimsical nature of human activity. Any economic transaction is in essence the meeting of one infinitely complex universe with another in the persons of the parties involved, with the resultant "price" being an expression of the economic ocean seeking its readjusted level. It doesn't necessarily look that way in the mundane pre-priced retail purchases that we engage in every day, but the process is there as a governing context. The GEM is a self-leveling instrument of veracity and precision that absorbs these interactions, as it reflects the vastly variable realities of the economic life. What could we even hope to be better?

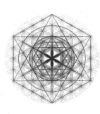

CHAPTER 9
INTEGRATION & SPECULATION

The Integration of Micro-Currencies into the GEM

A question naturally arises about how sub-national (micro) currencies might be integrated into the GEM. Within the basic scheme, each sub-national currency that showed up in a foreign bank would be tallied in a lump with its country of origin. The individual RCF's in the basic global matrix may, in fact, represent economic markets that are served by multiple levels of currencies. These markets themselves would be free to maintain their own domestic or nested matrices as represented by state, urban, county, regional or other jurisdictional boundaries. The regular normalization of such matrices would assure traders on the international market of each currency's worth. This is not to say that a unit of a local currency would necessarily be linked on a one-for-one basis with the currency of its nation of origin. Rather, its trading value could be made known in a very straightforward manner simply by publishing its respective RCF within its domestic matrix.

The associative floating nature of the GEM provides a naturally unfolding and seamless way by which individual micro-currencies can enter & leave the economy, and expand or contract relative to a lesser or wider marketplace. If a currency introduced into a very local trading zone were to gain acceptance over a wider area, it would at some point start to show up on the other side of a political demarcation that is represented in a currency matrix, whether local, state or national, and so generate another line in the trading matrix in which this demarcation is represented.

To illustrate, let us suppose that the Berkshares of the E.F. Schumacher Society in Great Barrington, MA started to show up on deposit in banks in the counties that bordered Great Barrington. This would, potentially at least, give the currency a trading value over wider areas of the state. It may or may not be acceptable to a potential trading partner outside its home county, but it would give those who might be inclined to accept the currency a basis on which to make their judgment.

The most likely "success" scenario is that Berkshares would gain acceptance in counties that immediately bordered the one in which Great Barrington was located, and then perhaps over a wider circle. The natural reference currency (RCF = 1) for a Massachusetts matrix would be the U.S. dollar. Therefore, the showing up of Berkshares in the state's trading matrix would give the currency an RCF, theoretically at least, with respect to the dollar. It is conceivable that given such a basis for determining trading value, Berkshares might gain a degree of acceptance in nearby New York, and begin to show up in New York banks. They would be identified as a Massachusetts-based currency, and its value would be computed on the basis of calculations related to the Massachusetts currency matrix, which would be linked to the domestic U.S. trading matrix, without requiring any particular regulation or legislation.

Conversely, if a micro-currency fell out of favor and ceased to show up across jurisdictional lines beyond threshold levels, it would simply lose its equation in the matrix, and revert back to being a strictly local scrip, or go peacefully out of existence altogether. This could all transpire with no disruption to the monetary order as a whole.

There is no particular limitation to how far this process could go, nor is there any particular threshold beyond which it needs to go. Currencies would be free to come and go for organically human reasons. It is likely that many sub-national currencies could emerge, but only a relative portion would gain wide acceptance. There could be minimum threshold levels of bank reporting established in the law to prevent this phenomenon from becoming a needless nuisance.

I would add a note here that, in a practical sense, what is needed to cross the threshold of acceptability that would actually cause a banker to be willing to accept a given currency for deposit is for it to be sanctioned in a substantive way by the social order in which its emission is rooted. This is a fancy way of saying that to be taken at a threshold level of seriousness, the currency needs to be redeemable for taxes. This would create, essentially, a basis for the currency in the law.

The emission of a local currency is potentially a valid way for any segment of the citizenry to empower its own economic activity without having to rely entirely upon outside sources. This is, in fact, precisely what happened in Massachusetts in 1690 when the Colonial Assembly became the first governmental body in the Western world to issue its own scrip as a fiat of the public will, which, in turn, became the virtually forgotten impetus for the

American Revolution. There is much that could be said on this subject, but not sufficient room to do it justice here. Suffice it to say that the civic redemption of local currency is a factor that, in my experience, is not given sufficient consideration in the worthy imaginings of local–currency proponents. This is not to say that redemption as taxes is strictly necessary to having a local currency, but without it, it is hard to see how such efforts can rise beyond being what are essentially coupons issued by various mechanisms as a promotion scheme for local merchants. There is nothing essentially wrong with that.

This is also not to say that for a currency to be acceptable for taxes, it must necessarily be issued by the government itself. After all the present U.S. currency is issued privately (but it behooves us to keep in mind that the arrangement has proved to be problematic). I just think that we need to be realistic about what is possible if whatever we use as currency does not have a root in the civic life of the social order.

The GEM and Multinational Banking

One might ask, would the GEM proscribe the existence of banking entities that straddled international boundaries? In my view it would not. A multinational bank would need to arrange its accounts such that the funds on deposit reflect in a bona fide way the political entity in which they are actually on deposit. They could not be simply lumped within the corporate structure of the bank in a manner that de-couples them from having to conform to the laws of the societies in which they are utilized. This would be an important factor in making sure that money serves, rather than dominates, the social order in which it flows.

We could also assume, disallowing for cash floating in people's pockets, that money-on-deposit was indicative of the actual areas where a given currency was being spent, and in what amount. The existence of cash floating in one country would tend to offset cash floating in another, so the effect of essentially ignoring this factor would be negligible. Any specific attempt to demand an accounting for it would tend to be intrusive.

The GEM – As Three-Dimensional Bookkeeping

My ignorance of bookkeeping is profound (hope to remedy that in the future), but I would venture a thought on it anyway. It strikes me that the mode of operation of the GEM would be symbiotic with the idea of money-as-bookkeeping. It would tend to draw the two-dimensional form of the balance sheet up into the third dimension, and renormalize factors at a yearly "closing". Beyond that, I would venture that money-as-bookkeeping is not the culmination of economic history, and that the GEM would be capable of acting as the perfect segue to what would follow. To be sure, this is an idea that needs developing, and a hypothesis that needs testing, but in principle it looks sound to me.

What Prevents the GEM from Working Now?

So let us assume that the Global Economic Matrix was recognized to be the inherent mathematical solution to the global trading order that it, in my view, is. Would that in itself allow it to work? I would say "yes", except for one problem: how do we account for the "interest" charge attached to the issuance of money within the current monetary order. With the loss of monetary value through payment of "interest" charges for which no value in a tangible economic sense is received, the simultaneous equations of the GEM can no longer be made to reflect reality. To be sure, one could still take an inventory of the amount of each respective currency on deposit in each bank on a designated day, but there would be inculcated into each total a major factor caused by the payment of "interest" which does not correlate with the value-added aggregates of trade in goods and services.

Under such a condition there is there is no solution set of RCF's which reflects reality. This, I presume, is at the root of why an array such as the GEM is never invoked under current conditions. What we get instead is this incredible chatter of financial sports talk which purports to analyze the problem and propose solutions, but in reality strains to finesse with ideological props, emotional gambits, fuzzy logic and media dazzle a situation that is structurally impossible to resolve from the get-go. This is at the core of how a whole world of presumably the most astute economists, financiers and politicians can put forth reams of argument that only dance around the problem in circles that spiral progressively away from any resolution.

Alternatively, for a domestic economy that uses a currency that is not "backed" by "debt" instruments, the fact that it can clear its own domestic marketplace of what it produces is true as a matter of course. This is not to say necessarily that its production is materially copious in relation to the population it serves, or that it is efficient with respect to its internal processes, or that it is self-sufficient in a physical sense so as to not need to trade for anything. It primarily means that the currency variables that are entered into the GEM represent the actualities of trade, and the system of equations has a bona fide solution.

The GEM and the Question of Currency Speculation

The question quickly arises – "Would the GEM be susceptible to being undermined by currency speculation?" My answer is that it would effectively preclude any opportunity for profiting from such manipulations due to several factors. The first is that such a system is constantly and transparently converging towards a stable equilibrium. It should be noted that the prospects for any sort of speculation depend on there being volatility in any market it would hope exploit. As outlined above, a "debt-money" system is inherently unstable. To avoid slipping into a contracting economic spiral, the people within it are forced to look abroad in search of opportunities for a "positive trade balance", or failing that, to "borrow" more money into circulation from whatever private cabal it has abdicated its natural power to monetize to. It is a classic Catch-22. This sets up a situation that resembles more nearly a perpetual bankruptcy reorganization, rather than a stable self-financing economic order.

The factor that fatally compounds the situation is that we, individually and as a people, cannot seem to admit to what is really happening. For many reasons we feel subconsciously that it is just too much to do anything about. The result is the creation of a massively convoluted cultural paradigm to maintain the lie. Lies themselves are fundamentally unstable, and require an ever-increasing investment in delusion to keep them going. Under such a circumstance the whole mindset surrounding money becomes a churning vexation. Financial markets, in turn, effectively degenerate into "group psychology". One has only to turn on the TV to behold the inscrutable "wisdom" of the stock market to see the result. This sort of effect covers the gamut of what might be called financial punditry throughout the public "dialogue". Within such an indeterminate situation people are extremely fearful, and susceptible to being stampeded by whatever specious "analysis", political bromide or half-baked economic theory comes along. It is within the obfuscation of just this sort of monetary miasma that speculation finds its green-velvet field of play.

Concomitant with the putative necessity of "borrowing" currency into circulation is the attachment of "debt"-based financial instruments to that money. These can take myriad forms, such as mortgages, certificates of deposit, derivatives, government bonds, etc. These instruments, in turn, are themselves bundled together and traded like so many gambling chits on the international market. Out of seeming necessity, consumers enter the fray in whatever way they feel competent to participate. This may take the form of shopping for interest rates, buying and selling goods on a speculative basis, re-financing one's home, purchasing goods before prices go up still further, buying stocks, hoarding, making heedless demands for future benefits at the bargaining table, and so forth. The whole of the life-economic structure truly becomes a casino where each player is betting to outwit the other, thought we strain to make it not look that way.

In such a situation the de facto ethic becomes get-in/make-a-killing/get-out. This is a far cry from the vaunted "work ethic", or a true entrepreneurial spirit that is willing to sacrifice to provide a good or service. The cultural moral compass becomes confused, then points south. The gamblers win and live in the Big House, while the suckers work and sink into "debt". Into the soft terrain of the American dream is cleaved a 'have-to-work vs. hold-speculative-paper' chasm. Some will say that this is simplistic, and to some extent it is, as there are still many out there who swim against the tide. I would even take it a bit further and say that most people in society struggle to occupy an economic niche they perceive as authentic, and not driven by avarice. Notwithstanding, we as economic players have for the most part already been sucked down into a negative monetary vortex.

As a way to cope, most persons in the society, to one degree or another, become speculators themselves. To be sure, we are loath to think of ourselves that way, and my experience is that most people are offended to hear of it (a flapping red flag in itself). They may be averse to speculation at heart, but they have to survive, and so imagine that they are obliged to play the game in some way to secure their just and necessary due. To illustrate how this can work, it is common for "regular people" to buy an obscenely priced house in the hope that they will get in on the housing-inflation balloon before it goes bust, and so reap for their pains a justly due profit. Few stop to think that by accepting, operating on, and even glorying in such gains as a social norm, they are essentially becoming speculators against the prospects of their own children, who will, as a matter of course, be the unfortunate blokes who will be obliged to pay the inflated price on an equivalent abode when they aspire to a home of their own.

We as a people are disinclined to call "speculation" what it is when it applies personally because we are not ready to come to grips with the unpleasant implications of the word. Aren't we, after all, just trying to survive in a game we didn't initiate? A subconscious duplicity of character sets in, and the delusions that cover it have to be constantly re-upped to maintain denial. If one were to think the problem out to its end, one would see that this becomes a moral cancer which eats its way into the joint-&-marrow of each person and all aspects of the culture. Even religion, for millennia the bulwark against financial speculation (usury), has largely succumbed. This sets up the veritable spell by which our whole civilization is becoming hollowed out.

The GEM would take the speculative margin out of the money markets because it would entail the recalculation at regular intervals of the normalized value of currencies as determined by actual value-for-value trade. Speculation requires the presence of a fog of indeterminable factors that can be leveraged and exploited. This is effected by the structural anomalies innate to "debt"-money, and the culture of fear and self-interest that it engenders. A system whose fundamental characteristic is to constantly converge to a stable condition serves to effectively squeeze out the "spread".

Finally, I would venture that a society that has effectively adopted on the personal level the ethic of money-serves-life, and established a usury-free monetizing structure in the political life, is almost by definition one in which speculative larceny has in the main lost its allure, victims, moral disclaimer, legal sanction and cultural glorification. I say "almost by definition" because there is still a possibility that we as a citizenry might not get it right (and wind up more vexed than when we began, but that is a topic for another treatise). Still, the quantum elevation of consciousness required to positively change the monetary system would tend to bode well for a life-economic transformation that of itself would preclude much of the tendency to avarice. We have no viable option except to try in any case.

To live out one's economic existence based truly on principles grounded in sound practices would of itself form a positive feedback character loop for the culture that would tend to reinforce itself over time. This would be in stark contrast to a perverse cultural inversion that effectively all but forces people to engage in de-facto larceny to survive, erects an edifice of denial to block any epiphanies that would permit us to see the proverbial pachyderm-in-the-room on the matter, and effectively generates and all-against-all mayhem of the social order.

In the ambiance of a true GEM, we might ultimately discover that much maligned "human nature" is not as corrupt as it has often been purported it to be. There are many examples in life of the natural predilection in human nature to act in a giving manner, if only it has the opportunity to act in an environment in which its innate altruism is not quashed, as when people are put in a position of not being able to pay their bills, or go into "debt" to obtain their necessities. If they cannot reform the system solely on their own recognizance, or even see the essence of the "debt" vortex they are caught up in, then they are driven to compromising their soul forces to rationalize living off their brother or sister. The impetus from that tendency, in turn, inculcates a spiritual decay that extends deep into the personal psyche and cultural zeitgeist in all areas of life.

In contrast, the very fact of the establishment of a usury-free monetary regime would be prima-facia evidence of a leavening of the whole. Within such a context, currency speculation becomes a pointless idea. I don't believe that this is too much to say, and we would do well to ponder this line of thought carefully to its natural end.

Through the GEM, transparency of the system is established. People could see where their money was coming from, where it is going, and how the ends meet. They would be empowered to make sensible economic decisions, at both the individual and social levels, from their own recognizance. They would no longer be vulnerable to siren calls of "balanced budget amendments", "paying down the deficit", "supply-side economics", "income redistribution", "running the government like a business", "cheap big-box pricing", "progressive taxation", and all the rest. Obviating such inanities would be the realization that money can indeed serve life "debt"-free in the context of an economic ocean that normalizes on a recurring basis to its natural level. This is the elixir of the Global Economic Matrix. In such a world the would-be speculator would have no option except to find a "real job", but that is not a problem. Possibilities for the social monetization of purposeful, satisfying and humanly empowering enterprise are endless.

CHAPTER 10
GEM & GLOBAL CONCERNS

The GEM Contrasted to a Single Global Currency

I recently downloaded and read virtually the entire content of the Single Global Currency Association (SGCA) website. From home to end it was packed with the most erudite analysis of abstract economic parameters. None of the dissertations made explicit reference to anything like the GEM, although I would argue that it is implicit in virtually all arguments. By this I mean there were frequent articulations of desiring to arrive at some just, equitable and stable world trading order. Indeed, that is what the whole global-currency exercise purports to be all about (sincerely I believe). I would assert that the GEM is the straightforward mathematical expression of that ideal. It is what a mathematician, scientist or engineer would invoke as a matter of course when confronted with a problem of "n" variables in "n" dimensions. There is no ideology in this.

The very idea of a single global currency represents a corralling of the economic means for structuring and animating world society within a single nexus of control. This is the very negation of the associative/self-leveling/holographic/ leavening power of the economic life. It is monoculture in a most virulent form, and the logic of the current perverse economic processes taken to their catastrophic end. Notwithstanding, current developments seem to be taking the world monetary order alarmingly in that direction. I am referring in particular to the trend for coalescing of national currencies into giant monetary unions.

The first was the European Monetary Union (EMU), with its issuance of the Euro to replace European national currencies. In addition there is a rising level of speculation in the media, both mainstream and alternative, which speaks of an impending North America Monetary Union (NAMU). As widely reported, it is initially conceived of as a merging the currencies of the U.S., Canada and Mexico into the "Amero" (presumably replacing the dollar), but such a union would likely expand over time to include Central and Latin American nations to the south. There is also increasing talk of the "necessity" for the East Asian block of countries to form their own union in response. Other regional unions are talked about as well, but the emergence of this prospective "big three" would effectively divvy up the global trading matrix on a trilateral basis.

This would no doubt create some immediate "efficiencies" that would for a time give the appearance that such a "streamlined restructuring" is "working", but because the system would still be based on privately-created "debt" money, the same stresses that created the "need" for a more consolidated regime would reemerge, though in a more acute and pervasive form. A great chorus would arise from establishment voices that the problem is that "the reforms did not go far enough". At this juncture the merging of the entire global trading order into a single nexus of control would be presented as one "logical" next step away.

It was disquieting to read the entire SGCA website and see so many economists and financiers who where ready, in one degree or another, to acquiesce to the supposed inexorability of this trend (to be sure, there were a few voices in opposition as well, but a mood of acquiescence and dearth of cogent arguments even from that quarter). To my mind this is a telling sign that we are in economic peril, and the window for avoiding monetary hegemony is closing. The antidote to this is a fully awakened consciousness as to the true economic sovereignty and potency of each individual, a concerted effort in the social/political realm to establish and implement a true "monetization picture", and the coming together by consensus of a world association founded monetarily on a GEM-like matrix. The very idea of a single global currency should be allowed to join personal avarice and monetary usury on the scrap heap of economic delusions that have proven to be inimical to life.

The Ability of the GEM to Transcend Economic Disruption

Within the GEM, unforeseen shocks to the world economy could be addressed with maximum alacrity. Let us assume, by way of illustration, that there was a natural disaster somewhere in the world that caused major economic disruption. An exception to the calculation interval could be made and values re-normalized based on estimated effects, say at mid-year. Errors in the estimates of any corrective factors would come out in the wash, so to speak, at the regular year end and subsequent closings. The ability to recalculate for exigencies imparts to the GEM an extraordinary flexibility to compensate for untoward economic trauma. Any real life breakdowns and stresses incurred could be met by a manifest human response, both from within and from outside the affected area, without undue regard to financial "affordability".

Under the current order, much of the "disaster relief" would typically consist of "emergency loans" to and "debt-restructuring" of the affected nation, and the adding of more "debt" to the already-in-the-red budgets of the donor countries. The ultimate assumed burden, of course, is underwritten by the taxpayers of both donor and recipient of countries. What is more, just like for any other usury-money injection, the "debts" so incurred initiate a snowball that will have to be rolled over ad infinitum. They will never go away, and so the whole episode will never be truly healed.

Contrast this to the response within a true Global Economic Matrix. Any financial adjustments occasioned by the "disaster" could be accounted for relatively instantly, and would in fact not cause a rent or serious imbalance in the economic fabric. This leads to a conceptual point that is important to take note of. The founding premise of a soundly constituted economic scheme is that the physical/human realities of life form the basis for the abstract monetary matrix. This monetary matrix, in turn, constitutes a mirror image of the life of the "real" economy. Furthermore, it is a spiritual axiom that, however roiled life in this world becomes on the surface, there is an underlying continuity within which spirit is still in control and all things go well. The fluid constancy of the GEM reflects that deep reality, and so can be said to be a true spiritual image of natural life. It inculcates an ultimate symbiosis of economic factors, which, in turn, creates an ideal training ground for the elevation of the spirit, which is what the meta-economic realm or the economic life should ideally be. This thought goes to dimensions of life that are difficult to describe, impossible to define, and transcend nominal considerations of monetary normalization embodied in the GEM.

The GEM and the Question of Tariffs

It is inevitable that in any discussion of international trade the matter of tariffs will come up. More specifically, how does the issue of tariffs relate to the GEM. Tariffs have been imposed generally for three reasons. These are:

1) Protect particular industries from foreign competition.
2) Maintain the general pricing level in the domestic marketplace
3) Raise revenues for the Federal government

In all the talk about "free trade" and "unfair trade practices", there has been a tendency to lose appreciation for the fact that the levying of tariffs has proved to be a useful, and indeed necessary, measure in the development of the major economies of the world. It might even be said those nations that managed to retain their political prerogative to impose tariffs are the ones that have evolved into the "first world" nations (the U.S., the major European powers, Japan, recently China), while those who did not (mainly because of a loss of political prerogative due to colonization) devolved into "third-world" status.

Speaking to point (1) above, from its beginning and well into the 20th Century the United States made liberal and targeted use of tariffs to protect its emergent industries. In fact, the second statute passed by the new American government was the Hamilton Tariff of 1879. The American philosophy on tariffs was summed up in an apocryphal statement attributed to Lincoln. When he was presented with the question of whether the U.S. should produce its own rails for the building of the transcontinental railroad, or import them at a lower price, he is reported to have replied - *"If we buy the rails from a foreign country, they will have the money and we will have the rails. If we buy the rails from ourselves, we will have both the money and the rails."*

Related to point (2), the U.S. has also pursued a general policy of maintaining tariffs sufficient to protecting the soundness of its own domestic marketplace. There have always been cheap commodities and manufactured goods available from slave-wage lands, whether from political colonies, or more recently so-called third-world nations. The American body politic has traditionally seen the wisdom in not permitting an influx of such wares to break the monetary parity in the domestic marketplace between production and consumption. In the last century, we as a culture have forgotten that aspect of our economic history under the influence of a withering onslaught of "free trade" propagandizing.

Concerning point (3), tariffs were the main source of revenue for the Federal government until early in the 20th Century. They have since been largely replaced by the income tax, which was ratified (arguably) in 1913, effectively in conjunction with the Federal Reserve Act passed the same year.

The question now is – "What is the proper roll of tariffs in this time?" The answer is that they are virtually no longer needed to fulfill their traditional functions. To understand this assertion, we need to assess the profound structural change that has overtaken the global economy. To wit, the world has been transformed from one in which nation-state economies maintained themselves behind political frontiers, to an integral global trading order.

For example, in the 19th Century the U.S. was a solitary economic entity afloat in a sea of other nations and undeveloped areas beyond its borders, with respect to which it had no control, but also relatively little need. Its most vital interest was in carving out a protected domestic space within which it could nurture its own development from its own resources. The main factor that could threaten that vessel would be a rupture that would allow its own good currency to drain out, and/or cheap foreign goods to flood in. The effect of either would be to deprive the domestic market cycle of the ability to balance its own production costs with consumer income. Some trade, of course, needed to be allowed, and this could be managed as long as the resulting inflow and outflow of monies did not cause a significant disruption of prices, and, in turn, the level in the monetary pool. The erection of a monetary levy around the domestic economy in the form of a wall of tariffs was the effective way to regulate the inflow and outflow to a level that would allow for the development of domestic industries. They insured that products imported into the country would have to be purchased in the domestic marketplace at an American price, and those exported would need to be bought for same.

While it is true, in fact, that there were frequently recurring periods of monetary trauma in the nation, these were caused mainly by internally generated stresses in the money supply, and so could be handled with internal readjustments, while the country as a whole progressed steadily ahead. Because America was largely self-sufficient in a material sense, and even then tended to be the higher-wage-and-price market, international trade resulted in a net source of revenue for the government which could be used as a sort of tax-collection system, the proceeds of which would flow into Federal coffers. This state of affairs persisted for a century-&-a-half as the result of certain differentials which existed between the domestic economy and the uncontrollable economic chaos beyond the national frontier.

So, where are we now? The frontier is gone and the world is now one economy. This is fundamentally true even apart from monetary reasons. The two great oceans are no longer insulating barriers. There are many strategic goods that we need from the world, and that the world needs from us. In the developed world, subsistence capabilities are largely gone. We have acquired foreign tastes, and foreigners crave American culture. There is emerging a densifying global communications web. People by the millions jet about the planet in mere hours, and patterns of immigration and ethnic exchange have transformed the American melting pot into a churning polyglot. Exacerbating this reordering is an extreme division of labor, which, in turn, results in a minutely fractured productive sector scattered literally over every nook and cranny of the globe, and the emergence of consumption patterns that are nearly as dispersed. We could argue about how good or bad all this is, or to what extent it is a result of a natural evolution, as opposed to being forced by political, military or economic manipulations (and indeed it is good that we have that dialogue as there are many lessons to be gleaned). The simple stark fact remains, however, that this is now one world, and there is no going back.

The germane question then becomes, how do we deal with being a one-world economy, as opposed to a collection of isolated economic entities nurturing themselves behind national frontiers? This requires an answer with many facets, but the topic of the moment is tariffs. In a global economy that has become unified, it makes little more sense to try to resolve trade issues by erecting tariff barriers between nations, than it would for states in America to create a tariff wall between Illinois and Indiana.

How then do we accommodate this overwhelming trend to one-world integration, and still maintain a sense of sovereignty, freedom and independence? The only answer I can see is to establish a worldwide Global Economic Matrix as the basic architecture for global trade. If one follows the arguments given in this treatise, I think one would find that this has the potential of preserving, and indeed actualizing, the virtues of being one world, while avoiding its horrific pitfalls. Not all the potential questions have been covered, or course, but that is all the more reason to have this discussion.

All this given, I would still not rule out the use of tariffs. A hallmark of the GEM is that each entity represented in the matrix retains (and indeed is freed up to exercise) full sovereignty and control over its internal processes. This means, by definition, that they could still impose a tariff on goods entering their economy. I would not be so dogmatic to say that this could never make sense from a domestic perspective with respect to some aspect of a given sovereignty's legitimate aspirations. An occasion might arise, for instance, where a people would for cultural reasons want to protect, say, a domestic wine industry, or nurture the growth of some particular manufacturing base. This is perfectly permissible, and would not cause a disruption of the GEM. It would only be incumbent upon a people exercising such an option to realize that any skewing of pricing thus incurred would as a matter of course be compensated for in the internal realities of their own domestic price structure, and whatever modification of trading patterns that this might engender would be reflected in the GEM. In any case, a tariff could be seen as a free creative option, and no longer as a weapon in the arsenal of economic warfare. Since the franchise to create money would be restored to the Federal government, it makes no sense to look to the tariff as a potential source of national revenue.

CHAPTER 11
TRANSITION SCENARIO

A Transition Scenario for Monetary Reform

It is one thing to build castles of a better world in the sky. It is another to put foundations under them. The world has survived until now virtually in spite of itself. Historically humankind could "afford" to indulge in its greedy machinations because the world was effectively bigger than what people could destroy in any final sense. There was always a frontier, both exterior and interior, that could absorb the excesses of human mayhem so that the seeds of civilization could survive to have another go.

By "exterior" I mean that there was always, at least potentially, a greater territory out there still to be conquered or exploited. It could serve as a compensating buffer for whatever internal inconsistencies an economy might embody. It could function as a source of distraction from problems at home, or a motivating bogeyman to justify economic measures that would otherwise not be acceptable (war is eminently useful on both these counts). It is a place where a despotic regime could export its problems, or even restive population if need be. It could serve as a refuge outside the existing order where a remnant might survive to reseed civilization in the event of economic implosion. Moreover, it constituted a potentially natural resource repository from which could be drawn the wherewithal to make a new cycle possible.

By "interior" I mean that in the past, even within the more evolved civilizations, there persisted sufficient subsistence skills and practice in the culture to tide over much of the population through extreme times. I am sometimes confronted with assertion that even if we had another "depression" we would weather it like the last time, and emerge stronger than ever. Let us take stock of the situation now. If the monetary system went down, the farmer would be in the food line nearly as quickly as the urban dweller, infrastructure and skills which formed the substance of the industrial sector have largely been transferred to slave-wage maquiladoros, and the technocrats of the post-industrial world would find themselves to be helpless babes with the high-tech teat withdrawn. In short, this is an unprecedented time in history. The world has turned over. We are collectively, all of us, out on one big limb, and even comparisons to ostensibly historic precedents still in living memory can be dangerously deluding. The exterior and interior and frontiers are substantially gone.

That this poses a life-threatening hazard is obvious, but it is also a marvelous opportunity. That is, it puts us into a position where we have to make the whole order work for everyone, from one corner of the globe (a peculiar idiom) to the other. There is no escape from others, nor from ourselves (nor from our Creator). It is alike in the truest interests of the most prosperous man of affairs and the most destitute denizen of the hinterland that this rectification go forward. Is it too much to say that the time draws nigh when this may be a life-or-death proposition for the race as a whole (I will let the reader decide that for him-or-herself)?

Generally speaking, economic and political ideologies have an implied death wish. On the right they are waiting for Armageddon to arrive, and seem bent on using the place to exhaustion like God intended before it happens. On the left they are waiting for the chickens of the evil system to come home to roost so their truth can be vindicated, not stopping to think that they are effectively longing for the pulling down of the pillars of the very temple that we all live in. There is a third way that purports to take the "high road" straightaway to sentiments of a new benign vision, but comes up short of conceiving of the bridge that must be built to get there out of the bricks and beams presently in hand. Finally, there is a subculture that has become obsessed with the gaping anomalies that are inculcated into the very foundation of the monetary order, and they are predisposed and able to research and publish scathing broadsides against the system, but their answer is typically to give up on the social order and sandbag their own position against the extreme times ahead. The rush to buy gold as a hedge is a common manifestation of this position. My analysis here is simplistic of course, as virtually all arguments partake of combinations of these tendencies, and no person is utterly deluded by, nor completely free from them. It is a struggle for all of us.

The question of transition ultimately rests on a two-step concept. On the one hand, it seriously behooves as individual souls to act upon connecting with the spirit in ourselves that would transform egoism to altruism. On the other, we would do well (with an active patience and without judgment) to look and work for the same leap of consciousness in each other, even in those deemed most diametrically in opposition. Many of my compatriots on the "left" argue that this is a naive delusion that keeps us from effectively going after the bad guys. Sure it would be nice, they concede, if "W" came to his better self, but don't waste your time on the idea. His ilk, so they say, only understands pressure of the political sort, and we had best be about putting on the squeeze. They lose sight of the fact that we share in every way a common humanity, and are in a sense all of "his ilk". We are also in need of correction and forgiveness on the matter if the full truth be known. This is not to proscribe engagement in political activity. On the contrary, such is a natural expression of a person's social predilections. We just need to not let our heads be turned by any tendency to think we are something that we are not. Humility, humor (especially self-deprecating) and circumspection before the truth should be our touchstone companions.

From the "right" side, great emphasis is placed on the inherent potential of the individual, and the idea that it is from this politically atomized being, with God in his corner, that any good we might do collectively has to arise. The contention is that it is foolish waste one's precious energy reforming such hopelessly corrupt things as "politics", the "government", the "monetary system", or social institutions at any level. These things will, so the thinking goes, take care of themselves when individual freedom and potential are sufficiently rewarded. I deem this to be effectively the "invisible hand" argument that is appealed to by conservatives of every stripe. It is particularly operative in "libertarian", "free banking", "free trade", "free-market", "free-enterprise", "buy-one-get-one-free", and other "free-most-anything" monetary arguments.

What it fails to sufficiently reckon with is that the "individual" has both a personal and a social nature. These are obverse sides of the same coin. Just as one side of a coin cannot be spent and the other returned to one's pocket, so is it impossible for a person to act individually without acting socially. Even if one withdraws deep into the woods to do one's own self-sufficient thing (I have literally been there), that withdrawal is in itself a profound social act. There is no way to be a responsible being except to be so on both the personal/individual and social/political levels.

There is a long history of morphic splitting of mankind's personal/social bipolar nature into dichotomous ideologies that may be described as right/left, conservative/liberal, individual/collective, etc. Politically speaking, these bifurcations are generally expressed directly or implicitly in terms that imply that we are inherently economically divided against each other. The effect of macro-monetary usury is to deprive the economy of the ability to complete its market cycle without being obliged to get the better of one's foreign neighbor, or failing that, to "borrow" from privileged interests that control the system. It is this fundamental dysfunction that is then exploited by the malicious spirit that would set brother against brother, or split persons internally within their own individual selves.

It also engenders myriad myopic stumbling blocks which influence those who would in good faith unite, to instead tragically divide. This sets up a situation where various segments of society are pitted against each other in a struggle to see who will have to go into "debt", be unfunded, remain unemployed, forego health care, or live in poverty to make the monetary ends meet. It becomes the means for setting minority against middle class, wage earners against the unemployed, labor against management, farm against city, black against white, the environment against jobs, state against Federal, liberal against conservative, individual against the community, citizen against government, and all other demagogueries of the bipolar tendencies of human nature.

We ought not repeat the mistake of dividing the question in our deliberations. Any transition strategy on the monetary scene needs to take the oneness of the personal/social or individual/political dichotomy fully into account. It must not make a false distinction between the micro and macro economic dimensions. It needs to address both polarities squarely, and not assume that one will in some vague way take care of the other. So the question arises, how should it be handled? The answer will be unique to everyone, but I would state it this way.

In the individual/personal arena, the case for change must be made in a manner that is not a personal attack, and yet challenges the spiritual inertia of everyone. It should be intrepidly candid and bracing, and cut through the "bs", so to speak, of everyone's opinions, ideologies and interests. It must express understanding for all, but quarter for none. It dare not be motivated by the prospect of hurting or offending anyone, but also not be compromised out of the fear (certainty actually) that one's message will be misunderstood. It should deal with denial head-on.

This is not to force the issue, as no one has to listen to one's message. Let the attitude be, rather, of a Cassandra, speaking one's

truth to whomever may hearken. The wake-up call may at times
bear a resemblance to preaching, but it need not be sanctimonious. It
is unmistakably "tough love", both with the other and oneself.
Indeed, that is the only way one can get away with a frontal
approach. People must be put fearlessly in touch with the fact that
they are the authors of their own reality. This is true in the economic
realm, as much as in any other, all appearances of victimization
notwithstanding.

In the social/political arena, the mind of an awakened
individual will naturally turn not only to how he can empower
himself, but also how that new awareness can be extended to the
wider family and community in which he lives. Institutional
arrangements are an inseparable part of that. Within this public
domain are included such things as foundations, corporations, the
government, the monetary system, and other artifacts of the political
life. Indeed, if a person's concerns did not extend to these, that
could be taken as telling evidence of an un-liberated self-absorption.

I have encountered many people who despair of the prospect
for reform in the public sphere. There is no one, they say, at the
helm of the economic ship. The financial life has taken on an
inexorable momentum of its own, and there is no politician, CEO,
banker, or anyone else that could effectively do anything about it
regardless of how much he might like to. What is more, things have
gotten so abstract, convoluted and pre-programmed that there is not
any effective way to deconstruct the system. Reform is a hopeless
task, so it is assumed, and we should tend to our business in the
personal realm. Things presumably will go better from there. To be
sure, there is much irrefutable evidence that could be cited to
support this attitude. I would, however, respectfully offer the view
that there is a higher reality to which the case can be appealed,
where social transformation and political reform is not beyond hope.
It is, in fact, eminently doable and strictly necessary.

Permit me to make the case. While it is true that no <u>personage</u>
is in charge, and 'money has come to do business on its own
account', it is also true that there has been elevated to lord and
master a perverse <u>principle</u>. In the micro realm I call that "personal
avarice"; in the macro "monetary usury", in the meta "globalism". If
the impulse for this negative tendency can be reversed in the micro,
then it follows that it can be implemented in the macro; and the
result will exfoliate in the meta. The micro and macro dimensions
are two poles of a spiral that reinforces itself depending on which

way the energy vortex turns. The imperative to reverse the "debt-money" mechanism <u>can</u> be identified, understood and acted upon. Anyone who understands cancer can see it. To identify a problem in the exterior realm is <u>not</u> ipso facto a blame game. Indeed, how could opposition to the usury-lion-seeking-whom-it-might-devour not be the impulse of an awakened soul?

But, it might still be asserted, what good would that do? The financial system is too complex, entrenched and bound up with selfish interests anyway. I would counter that while the monetary regime within which our economic life is enmeshed is indeed an impossible knot, it is a Gordian knot, and the overturning of usury is the sword that would cut it. Thomas Jefferson said, *"But follow the principle, and the knot unties itself"*. This is sagacious advice for our predicament. If money-serves-life were established as the operative principle of our monetary system, this nasty knot that co-opts our sovereignty and blocks our potential would begin to unravel quite naturally ("of its own accord", I daresay). What is more, the effect would extend into our personal economic lives in a process that is precisely the reverse of how the negative vortex came into being in the first place. This is not to say that there would not be a transition to manage, and expertise to bring to bear. On the contrary, the discipline of the financier would be urgently needed, but the impulse for the transition itself would rest upon a spiritual principle that all could comprehend. Properly conceived, it would not be an "expert" or "executive" decision.

The broad outlines of how this transition should be managed are straightforward. Under the current system, the "debt" paper backing the currency is turned in periodically for redemption. The way that "debt" is "satisfied" within the system is to forever roll it over with yet more money issued at usury, which only serves to compound the problem. In contrast, within a usury-free regime these instruments would be redeemed, not with more of their kind, but with usury-free public money, more on the order of Continental Currency, the Greenback or United States Notes. This process would necessitate the re-vesting of the monetary franchise in the national government and declaring all credits currently extant to be money. The authority to write these things came from the people through their government in the first place, even if it is a constitutional function that has been effectively abdicated to private interests through the so-called "Federal Reserve System". The monetary franchise is legally, structurally and morally out of place now. I see no problem in principle with restoring it as the political arm of the social order, which is what it should properly be.

From this point forward the money supply would no longer originate in "borrowing" at usury from private banks. Instead, there would be two primary monetization streams of emission in the public domain. The first would take the form of "spending" by the issuing authority (in this case the Federal government) of the money into circulation through whatever it purchased or paid out for the needs of its operations, or as elements of a social welfare base. It would be effectively vitalizing the outline of the "monetization picture" that society had composed for itself through its democratic process. Taxes at the Federal level would be a mechanism to draw excess money back out of circulation, thereby regulating the stream of the money supply injected via "direct spending" (or more properly speaking, "direct monetization").

The second stream would consist of loans issued interest-free to individuals, corporations and sub-Federal public bodies for enterprises deemed by the body politic to be most essential for society as a whole. Money quanta issued via this mode would be effectively controlled by the payback of loans. It should be obvious that both of these monetization mechanisms would be fundamental to the powers for economic self-actualization in the social sense.

For the duration of the deflation of the "debt" bubble, money issued to redeem the bonds issued against the dollar would effectively constitute a third and diminishing monetization stream that would automatically terminate with the redemption of the last bond. This would be in one sense a less-than-optimal monetization mechanism in that it would not allow for the same level of social control, but it would be necessary to deconstruct the old system in a systematic and orderly manner without trauma, default or recrimination.

Past injustices would in effect be recompensed by a deep justice in a transnational sense in that third-world peoples who have been supplying our material wealth for decades, while collecting mostly paper bonds and poverty for their troubles, would then be effectively holding coupons against the productive capacity of the American nation. As these were redeemed over the course of a generation, they would constitute the buying power needed for the people of their country to at last reclaim the fruits of their very real labors. Concomitantly, such demand would constitute the basis for rebuilding American industries in the course of paying this country's material debt. There would be a synchronous elegance and symmetry in the unfolding of this harmonization that relegates to inanities all the ostensible "free trading" schemes that are promulgated at present.

The establishment of these monetary streams would be instrumental in securing the "Social Welfare Base" (SWB) of the "Monetization Picture". This can be thought of as the segment of the economic pie dedicated to underwriting the human base of the economy. Putting it in a religious parlance, it would include among other things the social response to the commandment to feed the hungry, clothe the naked, provide for the widow, etc. It would constitute in-proportion (let me guess) half of the macro-economy, but likely significantly less with the generation of sufficient value beyond that required to provide a modicum of adequate and dignified maintenance. It would insure a level of life support such that people would in fact be poised to pursue their full potential without being intimidated by the prospect of social disempowerment, or pinned down by abject want.

There is a second piece of the economic pie that might be called "Private Enterprise Opportunity" (PEO). It would include a private financial market where interest would be a factor (but not usury). The critical distinction I would make on this wise between "interest" and "usury" is that the borrowing and paying-back of "interest" occurs within the context of money that already exists in circulation (and therefore does not deprive an economy of the money required to complete its market cycle), while "usury" is what is now deceptively identified as "interest" when it is attached to the "loaning" of money into the system (which in a practical sense shortchanges the market cycle, and guarantees the emergence of a vicious "debt" spiral). The PEO would comprise the arena where people would be free to act upon their beyond-subsistence potential ("liberty") in the economic realm. It would embody copious opportunity for personal development, expression and stewardship. The PEO is where people could find the means to "give something back". To be sure, it would also present some opportunity for avarice, but that is the hazard that must be endured to accommodate free moral agency. Besides, once out from under the morally corrosive influence and monetarily insatiable demands of macro-economic usury (attachment of a private "interest" charge to the money supply), human nature might prove to be not nearly as perverse and in need of micro-control as is commonly thought.

As to whether the prospect of overturning macro-economic usury is unrealistic, I would assert that it is the only realistic option. I say this partly because, whether it seems attainable or not, the situation in the world today demands nothing less. It is our "only choice", so to speak, if we are to avert implosion. Taking the thought further, precipitous transformation, I would argue, is the only way that real change has ever occurred. Witness the American Revolution. Who could have predicted that this disparate collection of people could have risen up out of their straights to challenge the strongest nation on earth, and take control of their destiny in a way that ran utterly counter to whatever in the world would have been deemed prudent, possible, or even thinkable? Notwithstanding the ever-present chorus of voices warning it can't be done, the consciousness of mankind has gone through many quantum leaps whereby what was incomprehensible one day became self-evident the next. At this "Armageddon-impending" juncture, how dare we entertain a transformation that is anything less?

One thing that stands in our way is the manner in which we have allowed the terms, conditions and parameters of our existence to be co-opted and burdened with impossible meanings. As an example, I would cite concepts which enumerate our powers in the public domain, such as "politics", "government" and "monetary reform". These have become so loaded that we run from them in despair. Yet, how can we believe in the efficacy of our better selves if we allow the fundamental institutions of our social selves to be wrested irretrievably from us? To say that we as a free and sovereign people cannot deal with our realities in the public domain is to say that we are insolvent on the social level, and ultimately the personal as well. I understand viscerally from personal experience the hazards of people's penchant for looking to some "government" or other external agency to solve their inner problems. As a political activist on the left for many years I have been as guilty as any of that delusion, and it took me some considerable time to mature (assuming I have).

Turning it over, though, I have also come to realize that a people that has reclaimed its sovereign power in the collective, is a people that, virtually by definition, has attained a quantum edification. From such an awakening, the outer manifestations (like monetary rectification) would naturally follow. Properly understood and practiced, there is no "statism" about it. All this is not to say that evidence of cogent reform is sufficient, but a lack of an impulse in that direction is telling evidence of continued spiritual slumber.

Taking the issue deeper, it is not only the "monetary system" that needs to be redeemed, but also the very language with which we think. Indeed, it might be argued that freeing the language, arts, science and other artifacts of culture is the prerequisite to any true reform. How, for example, can we expect to be sovereign in the public domain if "political" is a dirty word? It should be the operative word. Too often tagging an idea with the epithet "political" is enough to deflect the issue, and avoid rigorous thought. If something is too "political" it must ipso facto be corrupt - right? Why should this be? Who made it so? It would seem that the attempt to make it thus has been spearheaded by the malicious spirit that would deny the power of the social pole of humankind's personal/social nature.

It is true enough that "politics" can be problematic if not conducted with sufficient veracity, and that our practice of it has fallen to woeful depths, but to stretch that to the assumption that people have not sufficient power to conduct themselves in a ennobling manner in politics, the government, the monetary system or anything else is to say that they are bankrupt on the personal level as well. Where is the free moral agency in that?

Taking the argument to its ultimate end, I would say that "government", properly constituted and understood, is a truly "chaordic" body (i.e. chaotic and orderly at the same time). That it has been adhered to some partial interest is attributable to the fact that we as people have abdicated our power and permitted our sovereignty to become co-opted for purposes inimical to our nature. The economic root of this problem is that we have allowed money to rule, as in the form of personal avarice and monetary usury, and this in turn has driven all the pathologies of the system. If the monetary franchise were restored to its proper place, "government" would come to be regarded firstly as an enabling institution for the marshalling of human potential, and secondly as the agency charged with monetizing that potential.

The nature and dynamics of the governing process from bottom to top would be transformed to an extent that cannot be adequately described here. Suffice it to say that government would at last have the potential of becoming a truly effective body at the national level; rightly exercising by proxy the sovereign power of the people for purposes of enabling their true potential.

Integral to this, it would be widely realized that bona fide life-economic activity is the font of money, not a "cost". It is the very basis of the revenue required for financing (enabling) its own activity. This would be a revolution in consciousness (in a crucial sense the effective culmination of the American Revolution). We would witness a vast transformation from the chronic spectacle of partisan ideological bickering over a budgetary process in which it is assumed, preposterously, that a lack of money demarcates the limits of what can be done, while actual life potential, awaiting only equitable monetization, languishes inactivated because it cannot "afford" itself.

Having redeemed the money power through personal initiative, expressed politically through true monetary reform, the task remains of forming associations of sovereign entities in the global realm which will expedite the conditions within which the potential awakened can function on a symbiotic and mutually supportive basis. This naturally leads to the formation of an arrangement after the nature of the Life-Economic Associative Matrix.

CHAPTER 12
GLOBAL IMPLICATIONS

The Non-Invasive Character of the GEM

We have created a financial order that is bound up with the most incredible confusion of gimmicks, all in pursuit of an economic ideal that seeks self-leveling principles of structural soundness and economic justice. This ideal cannot be attained, of course, because the basic private-bank-loan transaction by which money comes into existence introduces a structural instability, and cannot serve as the foundation for a just and equitable order. But still we try. We have created a massive financial edifice constructed of patches upon patches, which include:

- The hugely invasive "progressive income tax code" (and the whole tax avoidance industry that has grown up around it)
- Ubiquitous programs of redistribution ("wars on poverty" in their many guises)
- The extension of sub-prime credit to those who could otherwise not get financing for their own home (and the measures to salvage the financial and personal wreckage left in its wake)
- "Foreign aid" programs (which morph into banker support systems at the expense of the ostensible aid recipients)
- Manipulation of exchange rates (as in the attempt of the Chinese to peg their currency at a fixed ratio to the dollar)
- Reactions against manipulation of exchange rates (as in the attempt to get the Chinese to roll back their fixed ratio, as if that were going to address the intractable reasons that made them feel impelled to be so adamant on this wise in the first place)
- Fantasies about if-only-we-returned-to-the-hard-money-of-the-gold-standard (forgetting the ruin such a policy has historically brought in its wake)
- Tariffs imposed in ways that are not appropriate in their place and time (which do little more than exacerbate the imbalances)

- Ever tightening financial security edicts (which transmogrify into smothering bureaucratic mechanisms and the Big-Brother organs of a "homeland security state")

This listing of well-meaning measures (and unintended consequences) could go on virtually ad infinitum. They are all essentially churnings of the financial system that fail to address the very impossibility of achieving their goals in a monetary order founded upon private gain at the expense of "the other" on the micro level, "debt"-based money creation on the macro, and international exploitation on the meta. This can all be reduced to one word; i.e. "U.S.URY" (as in "use-you-ery", or the practice of using you [my fellow human being] for financial gain). This would all begin to be resolved quite naturally and without undue stress (which is not to say there would not be a concerted effort required to make it work) in a monetary order based upon the sound principles inculcated in brother/sisterhood, true public money, and the GEM.

The universal upshot of all these misguided palliative schemes is that they are experienced in one's own life as being intrusive, increasingly to the point of abject oppression. All rely, in one way or another, on a tyranny of detailed reporting, capricious judgment, and micromanaging by agents of a system that has run amok. This is tempered by the humanity of the people that work within the system, but even they are losing the freedom to act upon their impulses as fellow human beings as their working mandates become ever more constrained and computerized. We are entering into a phone-tree universe where even the possibility of reaching a person or physically locating a party to deal with is becoming an anachronism out of the past. Just coping with the tax system is more that most people can reasonably accommodate. The rest is spiraling out of control, and our personal, national and world-community lives are being swallowed up by the inexorability of the trend.

In the world of the GEM, the problems that all these agencies of the "beast" are purportedly created to address would begin to resolve themselves back as closely as possible to the level of direct and transparent relationships between people (even if they are necessarily geographically separated). It avails the benefits of numerical calculations that are precise and meaningful to the n'th degree, but do not control anyone. Rather they float after the fact, in a manner of speaking, on the sea of the economic life. More remarkable still is that there is an almost total freedom from personal intrusion required to make the system work. There are no forms to fill out on a personal level that are inherent to the system. The numbers entered into the GEM are simple tabulations of "cash-on-hand" in bank vaults at regular intervals. Counting money is naturally what banks do already, so the reporting required for the GEM is virtually a snapshot of their ledger at a moment in time.

None of this to say that bureaucracy, forms or personal reporting would be a thing of the past. After all, we do yet live in an imperfect world. Such requirements would, however, tend to be scaled back to a level that was humanly meaningful and doable. In my own mind I carry an image of a world where such measures can, in the fullness of time, be done away with altogether. This is admittedly idealistic (many would no doubt say unrealistically so), but the matter does not have to be resolved at once. I certainly would not make any dogmatic assertions of what ultimately might or ought to be. The days work before us now is to rectify the economic order according to the providential evolution of humankind in its earthly sphere of existence at this time. With the Economic Life thus redeemed, we can safely trust the genius of our progeny to take it from there.

The Question of the United Nations & World Government

A question naturally arises as to the nature of any institution or institutions which would be associated with the GEM. More specifically, do we need a "world government" to administer it, and what would become of the present United Nations? How would world agreements and standards be enforced, and is "enforced" even an appropriate term for a free associative order? What would become of "free trade"? How would the operations of whatever mechanism that was adopted be financed? Would there need to be a world tax? These are questions that arouse heated debate even now.

We should first discover why the UN is apparently so dysfunctional in its current configuration. The root of the answer I believe is that it is laboring under an impossible condition. That is, it is the representative body of a world of nations which cannot complete their own domestic market cycles. To make up the shortfall its members feel obliged, therefore, to exploit their neighbors (i.e. gain a "favorable balance of trade") by whatever subterfuge is possible. To compound the problem, these nations are virtually without a clue as to the true nature of their predicament, and so act out their power plays within the most incredible ignorance and denial. It is a wonder that this organization hangs together at all. The fact that it does persist under such conditions is telling testimony of the determination of the world's people to try to work things out if only a way could be found.

If the world economic order could be established on the basis of a true GEM, then I believe that the way would be open to possibilities for associative initiatives and cooperation on a global level that are almost beyond imagining at present. In fact, they would evolve quite naturally and of their own accord, if only we could awaken the world to a more altruistic spirit, and excise the structural impediment insinuated into monetary systems by the influence of private "debt"-based money.

For purposes of this discussion let us dub this new world organization, of whatever form, the "Associative Nations" (AN). The name is aptly descriptive, and avoids the baggage that the moniker United Nations (UN) has come to be saddled with.

The question then arises as to whether the AN would constitute a "world government". It would not be a "government" in the sense that that it would be a ruling body. It could rather be described as an enabling body. It might in fact be composed of a number of institutions, themselves working together on a cooperative basis. Such entities might evolve out of current NGO's. The functions they would perform would surely include administering a Global Trade Registry to record the movement of currencies across borders, and plugging these numbers into the GEM.

There would presumably be a plenary body of ambassadors from each nation, or otherwise defined political grouping, where the basis for the resolution of issues would be consensus wherever possible, instead of the balance-of-power gamesmanship or the truth-by-legal-combat of a "world court". Much conflict could be avoided because, with the underlying subterfuge caused by structural indebtedness obviated, optimal outcomes could be realized in actuality. My guess is that this would work out better than we imagine from our present perspective simply because the supporting economic process would be transparently viable, and not of a nature that forces the "losers" (everyone ultimately) into "debt" in a downward-spiraling financial competition.

Other functions could include the setting of standards for measurements, the pooling of talent and expertise to address common problems, the enabling of global communications, diseases control and eradication, and other measures clearly in the interests of the global commonweal. It might even be reasonable to constitute such things as space exploration on this basis.

The question inevitably would arise as to the advisability and form of a military force to intervene in hot spots, or to protect the world as a whole against an aggressor. Terrorism would likely be greatly reduced or nonexistent, given that its causes would be profoundly ameliorated. If a threat did pop up, it is not armies that would be effective in countering it anyway, but rather the good will of the world's people (as our experience in Iraq should have taught us by now). Beyond that, if some megalomaniac did emerge (not very likely in my estimation) and entice enough people to follow, that is not something that would happen overnight. Any strategic threat takes time and resources to develop. Presumably, intelligent people would see it coming, and it could be handled on an ad hoc basis. The main preparation that would be required in advance would be a consensus on the outline of how such a contingency might be handled. Any standing "military force" would be more on the order of a public protector. It should not be a strategic force with offensive capabilities, as the very existence of such a thing would pose its own worst threat. At the max, any uniformed service should be modeled more on the order of the U.S. Coast Guard or National Guard in their public assistance and disaster relief modes.

The existence of an associative world body in the context of a viable economic order would be an unprecedented arrangement in human affairs, so there is a bit of speculation in anyone's view as to how it would work out. I would venture that within a properly constituted context, human behavior would need a lot less "governing" than we now imagine. We might in fact discover that cooperative activity is very much more in humankind's nature than we have assumed. The tendency for such may have been subsumed until now under the corrosive influence and bogus imperatives of an order founded on a corrupt principle. Wouldn't that be a marvelous discovery?

My argument here is in part simplistic. The larger reality is that we have lived, moved and had our beings within the imperatives of spiritual development all along. I am not imagining that our history in the earth sphere has been a sort of grand tragic mistake, or that there is anyone in particular to blame. We can presume that anything that has gone before has had its own reason for being. That does not mean we cannot study the past. It does mean that we can stop living in fear of its shadow. We would in a sense be at last free from it, and able to cast the light of our native intelligence into its litany to distill the many lessons it has to offer

Seen from a higher perspective, if a truly associative global order were to come into existence, that in itself would be evidence that the requisite personal and social transformations have already taken root. It will not have come from the micro as opposed to the macro domains, or visa-versa, but from a positive-spiraling action between the two. From there the possibilities become expansive beyond imagination. This is not as impossibly utopian as one might think. The entire transformation is only a turning of the spirit away. From there, words like "government", "political" and "monetary system" would lose their deleterious meanings, and be redeemed as resources of the language, as they are intended to be. There would only remain to do what needs to be done by people in the truth of the moment with what is at hand through social/political instrumentalities of, by and for the people.

The question soon arises as to how such a world organization could be financed. Would it mean having to institute a world taxing structure? I would answer that a world tax would be anti-ethical to a freely associative structure. A more appropriate solution would be for the AN to emit its own currency. It would be issued through spending to purchase goods and services required by the association to do its business, and be recovered from circulation through the invoicing for services to macro and micro economic entities that used its good offices. Remission could be paid in any currency because the normalizing monetary adjustments would be made through the GEM. This should work out relatively easily because the ability to pay for services without going into debt in the aggregate would be mathematically assured by virtue of the self-normalizing principle upon which the world monetary matrix was set up. Nations and other entities would be more that willing to pay because of the compelling benefits of having a harmonizing world system that functioned through a single nexus. Gone would be the divisive political battles over paying "dues".

This AN-issued money should not be confused with the notion of issuing a single global currency. It would be merely one sovereign currency among others which finds its equitable relationship to the whole through the GEM. Economically speaking this is very much in keeping with the presumed independent and impartial nature of the services the AN would render. I would recommend, however, that it be designated the reference currency for all others. In other words, this is the one that would be assigned an "RCF" of "1". The relative value of all others would be expressed in relationship to it. This would be more equitable than designating some "dominant currency", for example the U.S. dollar, as the baseline of reference; or an awkward scheme to rotate the honor between currencies. It would provide a convenient frame of reference whereby the value of each currency on the macro level, as well as each price on the micro, would be expressed in terms understandable with respect to the life-economic of the world as a whole. What could be more straightforward than that?

Into the Future

As a caveat I would add that what has been said above should not be construed to mean that macro-economic national currencies are any final answer to the monetary-reform question. They assume the primacy in the above discussion by default because of how the world economic order is organized at present. A check of one's wallet or bank account would readily show that the accounting chits are virtually all of national issue. This transition scenario is meant to address the redemption of the present order as a point of departure for an open-ended future. It is about, not the end of economic history, but rather a new beginning. From there anything is possible.

I would also hasten to add that this also does not preclude forms that resemble national currencies. The point here is that whatever steps are taken, they should leave the future unpresumed and unshackled. We may have our respective views about where this is all going or ought to go, but it behooves us to avoid the hubris of ruling out any possibilities from here. It is enough for now to rectify what we have in hand, learn from our experience in getting to this juncture, and leave the economic order poised for a new evolution into the future. In the long run, it is up to our progeny to determine how that will go. To contemplate anything less would not be in keeping with the ideal of liberty we espouse.

I would also note that when I speak of the macro-dimension of monetary affairs, this is not meant to be limited to the nation-state. The macro is in truth an aspect of the sovereignty that exists at all levels and for all groupings of society. To illustrate the point, the income of the breadwinner of a family is the macro-dimension of the family's economy, and the pattern of expenses, priorities and discretionary spending thereof constitutes the economic picture that it monetizes. This family enterprise, in turn, is a micro-fixture of the macro-pay-structure of the company within which that income is derived. This company is a micro-player in the state economy which is macro within its jurisdiction, but micro in relation to the national economy.

Naturally we could slice up the overall economic cake along many possible profiles. For example, there are at present nascent local currency schemes, such as Ithaca Hours. Generally, these represent true forms of money, providing they issue currency based on an enhanced margin of real economic activity which would not otherwise take place (much vaunted "frequent flyer miles", in contrast, are sales gambits that are already factored into the price of a ticket). What is more, they are macro-currencies with respect to the economic enterprise conducted under their aegis. They are also, at the same time, micro-currencies with respect to dollars. Ultimately, the micro/macro hierarchy is a fractal relationship.

The macro-dimension is a sovereign expression of any element of the social order that is able and chooses to expedite its good work by issuing a currency. The micro-dimension, then, consists of the body of players that use that currency. It should be understood that this cascading of monetary expression can exist along many lines of devolution. What is more, each "line" will inevitably be interpenetrative of every other one. This is not a blocking problem, however, because everything will be normalized in the GEM. The practical subjective factor about which a decision must be made is to set the criteria for drawing the line of demarcation that would determine which currencies are significant enough to be included.

One implication for the future in this analysis it that the composition of the GEM is open to modification subject to real economic change in the future. While the currencies currently in circulation tend to coincide with areas defined on the political map as nation states, that could begin to become less congruent depending on the evolving mix of participants. Non-state money issued by small groups, or even individuals, could be plugged into the GEM upon reaching whatever threshold criteria. Monetary matrices might even be nested in matrices, with the currency designated as the one assigned an RCF of "1" as the variable normalized in the higher order. The evolution of possible forms of the GEM is something that can be left open into the future. Ultimately this process could prove to be the effective vehicle for the evolution of a whole new world. I would not lay any rigid expectations of what that may look like from here, but the fact that it is open-ended and conceivable should be the good fruit of a viable transition scenario that it is our mission to accomplish now.

CHAPTER 13
TRADE WITH CHINA

The "China Problem"

Both the U.S. and China are caught up in the same usury-based world monetary system. The nation, relatively speaking, that bears the most responsibility for that state of affairs is the U.S. This arrangement was sealed at Bretton Woods, and in actuality has only grown more entrenched and pervasive since then. It would seem logical, then, that it is up to this nation to make the first move to remedy the situation. To bring a sound and just monetary order into this world is, in my view, a providential task that has been bestowed upon this nation since before the American Revolution; at least since 1690 when the Colonial government of Massachusetts became the first in the Western world to issue a paper currency directly as an emission of the sovereign enterprise of the People.

The steps necessary to fulfill that providence are, as best I can discern them, outlined in the above treatise, the Iraq War open letter, and others of my writings. I invite others to join in with this dialogue.

In the same manner as the U.S., the Chinese cannot complete their own domestic market cycle. They too must look to a "favorable balance of trade" (an oxymoron if one thinks about it; there is no favoritism in balance) to cope with their situation. This is bound to be true regardless of whether their leadership is ruthlessly totalitarian or benignly democratic. This is not to say that there is no distinction between the two. We must recognize, however, that the first law of economics is *necessity*. Whoever is in charge is obliged to pay heed to it.

It is also true that China is a huge and venerable society that is undergoing wrenching changes. In real physical and human terms, its problems are mind-boggling. There is, without a doubt, transpiring in their cultural/political/economic order a life-&-death struggle between forces of the dark and the light. The severe conditions and delusions under which it labors can only be exacerbated by the obligation of having to emerge within the toxic economic environment of a global monetary order that is based on "debt". I can image that this effectively forces souls striving from a more beneficent spirit into the clutches of the more sinister influences. The arena of monetary redemption is where we as a nation can help most. Indeed, it is our providential task to do so.

China needs to import virtually all its oil and many other raw materials. They have a massive population, but are losing the agricultural basis for feeding them. Ruination of the air, land and water by pollution, depletion and mal-development is pervasive. Sheer crowding is taxing their living space. Is it any wonder that they feel compelled to gather in U.S. dollars, the "paper gold" which backs practically all international trade, to cope with their own inherently vulnerable position?

Chinese confidence in the bonds they purchase which underwrite U.S. debt is no doubt becoming untenable. Still, for reasons that are complex, they (like much of the rest of the world) feel it in their interest to continue buying them. This self-interest may be morphing into a worried desperation, as they try to protect the soundness of their own monetary position. There is much talk about switching to the Euro, Yen or other reserve currency (even the Renminbi), but no one knows how to make the leap without triggering a world financial catastrophe. That said, the day is fast approaching when their hands may be forced. What that would look like is anybody's guess, but the fallout from such an eventuality is surely something we would not want to contemplate. The tragic upshot is that such a gesture might be futile in the long run anyway. Any currency that the world could make the switch to currently suffers from the same usury-based structural deficit. It would only be a matter of time before it too was as bound up with "debt" as the dollar is at present.

The China Solution

But there is a solution. If the dollar were no longer a "debt"-based currency, the global monetary order would be transformed. This is a sweeping statement to be sure, but I believe that it can be shown to be justified. Among other things, the complex and paradoxical problems associated with the Chinese hoarding of bonds backing the dollar would begin to rectify themselves virtually of their own accord (*"But follow the principle, and the knot unties itself"*). The first step to accomplish this would be to establish the dollar as a public currency emitted interest-free out of the U.S. Treasury. There is no legal barrier to doing this, as Lincoln's "Greenback Act", augmented by the Agricultural Adjustment Act of 1933, is still in effect.

With a change to public money, monetization of the U.S. economy could be implemented via two streams. One would be for money to be loaned into circulation (much in the manner that it is done now), but not at interest. Its level would be self-regulating via the loan-approval-and-payback process. The proceeds would go primarily for purposes that benefit the commonweal, public infrastructure being but one example. The other monetization stream would be direct government spending. Its level would be regulated through the taxation and retirement of any excess buildup in the monetary pool.

As for the bonds "backing" the dollar, most of these are now held by foreigners, increasingly the Chinese. The announcement that the U.S. was going off the "debt-money" system would signal that the bonds already extant are the last "interest"-yielding instruments of the sort available. The pervading worry that they are the air in a "debt" bubble that is destined to one day burst would be instantly rendered moot. Indeed, these bonds would suddenly become secure interest-bearing instruments of limited issue.

Those possessing them would naturally hold them to term, and that would work out just fine because it would set up an orderly process whereby they could be redeemed over time for United States Notes ("Greenbacks"), instead of Federal Reserve Notes ("debt"-based currency, for which there would be issued more bonds). The debt-spiral would be effectively halted in its tracks without trauma or default. These outstanding bonds would suddenly become what are essentially claims against the future productive capacity of the U.S. The only thing the Chinese government and top financial interests holding these bonds can do is to cash them and spend the dollar proceeds as they reach maturity.

From the perspective of the Chinese, these bonds are essentially transformed from being "debt"-bearing instruments that the country is obliged to hoard to underwrite their own buying power in the international marketplace, into a reserve that it is free to cash in and spend as they reach maturity. For years, the value of what the Chinese worker has been creating with his or her own hands has been siphoned off into these foreign bond holdings. Now it can be redeemed in the U.S. marketplace as genuinely-earned, but long-deferred, purchasing power. This would inculcate a profound element of justice that is due the Chinese people. Concomitantly, it also constitutes a currency stream that could help to rebuild the American manufacturing capacity lost to China in the first place. The initial influx of money would tend not to be inflationary since it would stimulate a commensurate level of economic activity. In the long run, any buildup of currency that did turn out to be excess to market requirements could be taxed out of circulation and retired.

As a final note I would offer a thought about the question of technology transfer to China that could be used to threaten this nation militarily. The United States has been since the end of the Cold War the number-one arms exporter in the world, and much of this materiel has been used against us, either as threats, or in actual combat (who armed the Iranians under the Shah, Saddam in Iraq and the Taliban in Afghanistan?). Clearly, it does not make the world safer for the U.S. to fill the planet, supposedly teeming with terrorists, with weapons we cannot control. The stealthy transfer of technology to the Chinese can only compound our security problems. The question has to be asked, what is so compelling about this sort of enterprise that our nation can't resist it, whatever the security implications?

The vain ambitions of university professors and venality of government officials may indeed be a factor, but I think that the problem is more fundamental than that. Why does this country compete in the international arms market at all? I have often heard expressed an underlying resignation to the idea that our country "needs the jobs", but in my view, that is a euphemism for it "needs the foreign exchange credits". That rationale would not exist if our economy did not constantly experience a felt need to halt the slide into "debt" in the balance-of-trade game, which "need", not incidentally, is an extension of the inability to close our domestic market cycle, which at root arises from the "interest" attached our money in the private bank "loan" transaction by which it is created. Clearly, there is a chain of cause-and-effect at work here that is driving the military transfer phenomenon in a senseless direction. I don't know if monetary rectification would entirely halt the race for market-share in this lethal "trade", but clearly it would remove a lot of fuel from the fire (my best guess is that for a totality of reasons, such commerce of death would end).

A New Future for China and the United States

As a world humankind needs a new future. The ones we can imagine now seem to be shadowed by dark clouds that no one knows how to dispel. The American mindset is haunted by a fear that arises from the very specter of a nation the size of China attempting to emerge into the modern world. "Oh my God, what if all those Chinese want to live in big houses, drive cars and live the "good life" just like we do? The earth is buckling under the weight of our own consumption now. How does this not turn into a life-or-death, superpower-against-superpower, struggle to survive in a time of post-peak oil, global-warming and disease pandemics (e.g. Chinese bird flu)? Perhaps we can sign a treaty whereby they will agree to limit themselves and not be a threat to our lifestyle". These arguments are not subliminal. I hear them voiced in the media, and not only on talk radio. Clearly we and the Chinese need a more adequate vision for the future. The question arises, then, "On what basis could it be hoped for?" In a practical sense, this must begin by examining the mode by which money is created, issued and controlled.

A key factor in the private-bank-loan process is that for a loan to be approved, someone must put up "collateral"; i.e., tangible property or economic activity to "secure" the loan. We have also seen how a society which is tethered to a "debt"-money system is obliged to go deeper into debt on a continuing basis. This is another way of saying that it must find a way to put up more collateral all the time. The way this works out is that the size of the economy in material terms must basically double once per generation (24 years at a net 3% growth rate). One is obliged to consider how long we could hope for the economic activity of the planet to be materially supportable if it is forced to re-double every twenty-four years, against a continually diminishing resource base to boot. It should be noted that this imperative is dictated by the mathematical "need" to service the compounding "debt" against the money supply, quite apart from actual human needs.

The "bottom line" is that in the end the 'debt"-based monetary system tends to drive the evolution of life in a materially snowballing direction. It is mainly the quantification of the material that is the basis for collateral. It is true that this has become modified to an extent in that value in the material world is now interpenetrated to an ever greater extent by intelligence patterning. This is the reason why, for example, my father used to crunch out the math for his business laboriously on a ten-pound metal adding machine, while now it is possible to hold in the palm of one's hand a device in which is inculcated immense computational intelligence that can be programmed to handle every aspect of one's bookwork comprehensively and literally at lightening speed. Clearly, we have become vastly more "productive". Why, then, was it common for those in my father's day to work one job, buy a house, raise a family (five kids in my father's case), allow the mom to stay at home, and still have a good life, while in this vastly more "productive" era it takes two incomes and no kids to subsist in an apartment?

The answer for this, of course, is complex, but I would suggest that at the root of the conundrum is the usurious nature of money, and the "interest" cost that is at once driving life in the direction of endless material expansion, and ultimate financial un-affordability. This dilemma seems to be the besetting preoccupation of almost everyone I know, and its effects are visibly decimating the earth around. To have any prospect for a viable future, this riddle of having materially to double and redouble just to meet cash-flow, and then not being able to afford it (vast productivity gains notwithstanding), must be answered even within the economic life of America. How much more imperative then, must it be to come to grips with this uber-catch-22 in a world burgeoning with billions of emergent people in China and elsewhere? Life does indeed still hold the potential for expansive growth, but its multi-dimensional reality cannot be realized until it is freed from the slavish ersatz-necessity to forever compound its material-exploitation base to satisfy the demand for collateral to secure bank loans which cannot ultimately be paid.

There is, as I write this, news in the media that raises a question as to whether our world is now in actually approaching the point where the physical/human realities of the economy can no longer keep up with the mathematical fantasy of endlessly compounding monetary "interest". How, then, can the present cancerous financial model be the basis for a world that has to move into the future, while accommodating the needs and aspirations of a billion-plus Chinese (plus billions of others)? Clearly, we need another vision, and a new way forward.

The practical first step is to return the money-creation process to the public domain. The salutary effects of this measure would be manifold, not the least of which is that what we do economically would no longer be driven by "debt". Instead, the money supply could be increased or decreased according to whatever was available and required at any given time. Activity that was heretofore deemed "uneconomic" because it was not suitable as collateral for "debt" could now be performed.

For example, gleaning the landscape for recyclables, cleaning up the air and water, reclaiming the land in a healthy way, alternative energy, appropriate scale of enterprise, keeping a parent home to raise children, authentic lifelong education, holistic health care, good food, and whole new rhythms and patterns of life would now become not only "affordable", but logical. The natural rhythms of life, which have been annihilated by the relentless demands of the monthly payment plan, could at last resume. Such an economy would not be forced to mindlessly "grow" irregardless of all other factors. Rather, it could expand, contract and transform itself according to actual needs, without financial trauma or default.

To be sure, this is a big vision, and there is not room to develop it here. What I do suggest, however, is that such a monetary rectification could be the basis for a shared new frontier for a global cosmopolitan civilization. It would open a way to supplant competition, obsessive material excess and mutual ruin, with cooperation, multi-dimensional growth and mutual enrichment. The fact that we have potentially in China such a large, creative and energetic partner in this quest should only bode well.

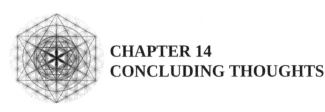

CHAPTER 14
CONCLUDING THOUGHTS

The Global Economic Matrix (GEM): Its Holographic Nature

The nature of the Global Economic Matrix (GEM) is holographic. If one pours a bucket of water into the ocean, every molecule of water in the ocean is obliged to adjust itself to that single bucket, and the water from the bucket must accommodate itself to the ocean as well. In effect, the whole becomes an expression of the part, and the part becomes a manifestation of whole. This symmetry is one of the fundamental properties of holography. The parallel with the GEM is a near perfect fit. The quintessential elegance of this concept opens up a whole universe of economic contemplation, the implications of which can be only be hinted at here. The shift from a money-over-life paradigm to an open-ended future where money-serves-life truly transforms the analysis, dialogue, story, mythology, dynamics, and other aspects of life in an all-encompassing manner.

For a contrasting "reality", tune into virtually any economic discourse at present (whether in print, over the airwaves, in texts, or wherever) and one is subjected to what might be called "financial sports talk". This metaphor comes to me from watching the spectacle of TV stock-market reporters on the trading floor breathlessly trying to make some sort of sports-talk-like drama out of the capricious trends they are obliged to sort through as the source for their subject material. It purports to analyze all the factors affecting the economy, how they play out in the economic indicators, what players are pulling which levers to right the economic ark, who the "winners" and "losers" are, etc. This strikes me as folly. It is akin to a physical scientist proposing that the oceans can be controlled by manipulating and second-guessing the nano-reactions between the molecules that constitute its body.

Pundits who purport to analyze financial trends are enamored of the notion that the adjustment of one economic indicator can create more-or-less predictable effects in another. To solidify this predilection they have embraced some "laws" and practices that I find to be of dubious veracity. In the jargon of economics, these include the techniques of "ceteris paribus", the Latin literally for "all else equal"; and "Ockham's razor", or the cutting away of all factors ostensibly extraneous to the question. Another specious device is the ubiquitous Cartesian graphic that purports to represent visually two economically representative factors on opposing axes in the manner in which they are ostensibly related to each other. The best-known example is the "supply-&-demand" curve, but there are many others.

One particularly bizarre rendition I can recall from the *Economics 101* course was when the professor drew on the blackboard something called the "Production Possibilities Frontier Curve". The supposed purpose of this exercise was to illustrate the limits of production for a hypothetical economy as affected by the playing off of two products against each other. In this case he drew a graph with pantyhose on one axis vs. tanks on the other, the premise being that this represented a hypothetical economy whose only potential products were pantyhose and tanks. The idea was to illustrate that if a society were to dedicate all its productive capacity to manufacturing pantyhose, it could not produce any tanks, and visa-versa; but if it decided instead to divide its productive capacity between the two options in varying proportions, that would result in possible economic output totals represented by the shape of the resulting curve.

To imagine in this manner that when one economic indicator is changed, it produces a predictable response in another is tantamount to thinking that if one dumped a cylindrical bucket of water in the ocean it would sink as a un-dispersed unit into the body of water, and be compensated for by a bucket-sized liquid cylinder popping up somewhere else. That this is an absurd premise at best should be self-evident.

To be fair, those who invoke such devices would be quick to counter that they are only illustrating a principle, and should in no way be considered as looking at the matter so simplistically. I would be obliged to concede a point on that. Further, I would stipulate that I don't necessarily proscribe the use of such abstract devices. There are, after all, limits to all analogies, metaphors, imagery, and words themselves. What could be said without them?

The problem is that when one is working in a field of inquiry which cannot arrive at solutions due to a hidden structural anomaly that has no way of being compensated for (as for example in an economy into which a cancerous usury charge attached to money creation has been insinuated), a peculiar reverse-alchemy takes place in the thinking process whereby the manipulation of such factors comes to be regarded, not as abstractions that illustrate an intellectual point, but instead as controlling parameters that determine "economic forecasts". The defect compounds itself into a veritable froth of "financial sports talk" that passes for sober analysis. This becomes so ingrained in the culture that even the best-&-brightest among us (and I say that without irony) can lose the ability to see out of it. Out of this womb of befuddlement, the through-the-looking-glass world of "financism" is born. Its very existence depends on remaining in deep denial about the holographic nature of the life-economic, the distorting effects of usury attached to currency creation, and the fact that changes occur in the body-economic only as a whole (just as the ocean inevitably changes as a whole when that bucket of water is added).

The upshot of this illusory state of the economic art is that the factors orthodox financial analysis purports to weigh are essentially phantasms. Far from being the levers that guide the life-economic ship, they are in actuality straw men, euphemisms, and double-speak for the monetary dysfunction of a system based on "usury" attached to the issuance of money. This is an audacious assertion, to be sure, but it is possible, in my view, to run down the gamut of econo-speak and demonstrate that this is so. All this is not to say that financial stewardship does not have an essential role to play, but this should be practiced in a manner consistent with the self-leveling nature of economic life as expressed individually through the productive fruit of personal enterprise, structured equitably through a sound macro-monetary system, and related associatively in a Global Economic Matrix.

The wizards of finance would do well to give up the hubris that they are pulling the strings on life, especially when their abstract indicators are almost totally bereft of real-life factors. While it might be fairly stated that money has come to do business of its own account, I would aver further that finance has come to do thinking of its own illusions. These phenomenon are linked, and it is the bondage to shadow concepts in an ersatz-financial realm that, as much as anything, prevents liberation in the monetary universe from happening.

From a general inquiry, it appears that the emerging model for the new vision in all phases and disciplines of life science is holographic (three-dimensional; the whole implicit in every part; a transcendence of the divine and the profane), as opposed to a flat picture (two-dimensional; each fragment carries only its own information; projection of white-noise light through flat pattern). I took a class in holography at a local university to gain metaphysical insight into what the phenomenon represents. As part of the coursework we were able to actually set up and photograph holographic projections of small objects. It worked pretty slick.

The setup is something like this. One starts with a source of pure synchronous light (a laser). The beam is split, with one-half falling on the physical object being projected. This object beam results in a reflected light pattern that is essentially chaotic, with no decipherable information in evidence whatsoever, until it is directed to intersect with the as yet pure half of the beam. The resulting interference pattern is the holographic projection. What is more, the entire holographic image is (unlike for flat film) encoded in every fragment of its whole. This has many implications as a model for reality. I am reaching for an analogy here for the relationship between the wild disorder in our mundane lives and the perfectly coherent light of the divine. The dynamic analogue of our lives is a seeming free-thinking/feeling/willing chaos (it is not just code), until, that is, it intersects with the pure light of its source. This generates a form that is a true manifestation of the real-life object in this plane of existence, but on a rarified level.

This concept can help us understand the economic life in a deeply existential way. First let us take a look at the personal dimension. Notwithstanding whatever outer monetary dysfunction may exist in the world, there exists for each person every possibility of being one of the "winners" in the economic game (let us say, a member of the top quintile that supposedly holds the lion's share of the "wealth"). "But for grace", as the saying goes, any one of us could also have been one of the "losers"; or worse yet, so abject that the very notion of winning or losing would exist in an abstract universe beyond the pale of any practical reality in our lives (which is where, lest we forget, billions of people in the world are forced to exist and still attempt to retain their humanity). For all our carping about the "monetary system", the ruling financial force in our personal universe is a hidden (karmic? providential?) hand that fixes our position in the spectacularly capricious firmament of possibilities, which, one is forced to admit, is out of the range of any final ego-hedged control (which is what makes it scary). At some level then, all our complaints about usury, the Fed, the government, corporate predations, or whatever are really just projections of that inner ontological travail that keeps us suspended in whatever fiscal purgatory we are wont to occupy.

I am reminded of the character in the movie *What the Bleep* who attracts the spill on her dress. It is to all appearances the most happenstance of occurrences, and yet it obeys (according to the film's premise) a reality that she on the "quantum" level chronically projects. Perhaps our relationship to money in our respective individual universes is something like that. Such a causal relationship is not hard to concede in the amorphous abstract realm, especially for we spiritual dilettantes, but it is different when it is stubbornly personal, which money always is. It would be interesting to contemplate doing a "Bleep" film on the quantum metaphysics of money, and how our habitual monetary circumstance finds its source in the unfathomable innerness of our being. Surely we would discover that our collective systemic dysfunction originates from there as well. That would be a story worth telling if one could find the wit to understand and the artistry to express it. Our personal lives are in a sense extended monetary moments of truth. It is easy to give glib back-talk about how to change the world, but hard to realize answers about how to resolve the personal quantum self that projects that world.

One way the conundrum can be modeled is to imagine a pure light of the spirit which when manifesting through a human being is essentially bifurcated, with (#1) one portion remaining pure, and (#2) the other a chaotic beam resulting from its reflection off the riot of complexity, perturbation and contradiction that is the personal/individual human psyche. While this reflected beam is scrambled beyond deciphering, when it reunites with the yet pure light of the spirit, the result is what may be termed a (#3) hologram of the soul. This three-dimensional chimera is at once a non-substantive phantasm, and yet eminently real manifestation of our total self. It is in this sublime construct that the indefinable existence of our personal economic life as described above resides.

This would seem to circumscribe the economic question, but the truths of life are all ultimately paradoxical. There is also a social/political obverse to the personal/individual side of the economic-life coin. The process by which it manifests is similar, except to say the body that the spirit beam reflects off of is a collective one, and entails among its parts the social arrangements, political institutions, corporate entities, and even intellectual paradigms that are manifestations of that dimension. It embodies chemistries of relationship that are beyond description. This produces a veritable hologram of which the economic life of any given cross section of souls is manifested on its indeterminable, yet ultimately deterministic, level. We can see this, for example, in the characteristic life-economics of the various nations, classes, occupations, regions, and whatever other groupings.

Ultimately these two holograms themselves generate the (#1) micro-economic and (#2) macro-economic dichotomies that give rise to the sovereign social entities that constitute the world economic community as a whole, whose patterns of intercourse generate the relative values represented by the variables that are arrayed in the GEM.

To take this idea a bit further, I would note that the respective (#1) micro and (#2) macro dimensions themselves represent cardinalities of triune holographic manifestation, as enumerated immediately above. What is more, they are expressions of the (#1) personal and (#2) communal aspects, which in a worldly sense are commonly portrayed as being at odds with each other (which is the basis of virtually all left/right political ideology at present), but attain a unity within the circle of the whole (as represented by the GEM). The metaphysical implication of this is that if we were to lay the oppositely oriented micro and macro triangles over each other within the unity of the GEM circle, we would have the economic representation of Solomon's seal. We would also have a graphic representation of the number seven, which is the number of completion in creation. If we would be as wise as Solomon, perhaps we should know this.

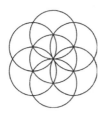

*All this should at least suggest that, though the concept is deceptively simple, the implications of the GEM are vast. My feeling is that **the pattern it represents** would constitute a worthy basis for contemplation and implementation of an economic life that was transcendent in its manifestation. - Rich*

*Thank you, and I look forward
to further discussions on this topic -*

Richard Kotlarz

richkotlarz@gmail.com

ABOUT THE AUTHOR:
BRIEF BIO & AUTOBIOGRAPHY

Brief Bio:

Richard Kotlarz has worked for over 20 years as a technician in the fields of engineering consulting, industrial testing and product design. He has combined this with a wide range of other life experience, including military service in Vietnam, work in human services, political activism, and the building of a deep-in-the-woods earth-sheltered homestead. His background, however, does not include significant professional experience or academic credentials in the area of economics. He has, rather, come to his interest and learning in the subject as a common citizen with a personal mission to understand and resolve the larger issues in the world around him.

This has produced a unique approach to economics, as well as other subjects, which is rooted in intuition and common sense. It challenges the assumptions of both orthodox and "alternative" discourse from the outset. He is currently involved in efforts to distill the fruits of that quest in a number of outreach efforts, among them the making of a box-office movie that will lay bare the emperor-has-no-clothes heart of the perverse monetary principle which is consuming the world and all the life in it. To be sure, this is deep and unflinching in its look at all this implies, but it is not Armageddon mongering (though it does not dismiss dire perspectives). It is in the end a turning over of the question, so to speak, to reveal a breathtaking new vision on the other side.

Autobiography, with philosophical background:

Nominally, this is a treatise about economics and money. In reality, it is a step in a very personal journey. I have no qualifying expertise or credentials in the subject. My resume "boasts" two college intro courses in economics, a marginal business of five years duration, virtually no financial estate, and bad credit. My foray into the subject began with only native intuition and a childlike delight in discovery. One who approaches the study of an established discipline from such an angle ingests over time the same points of knowledge as the on-track student, but his understanding is not necessarily ruled by the orthodox assumptions that are dictated by the gatekeepers of the craft. There is a native discernment developed whereby the founding "truths" of the discipline are not swallowed whole, but scrutinized as to whether they indeed are truths. This can make all the difference.

I am a quintessential baby boomer and child of my time, and this inquiry is an intensely idiosyncratic expression of that identity. I have always been a person of intense mental activity with a consuming interest in diverse aspects of life, and have tried to live that out in a '60's-and-beyond personal quest. As one who kept faith with the spirit, though not the excesses, of the Cultural Revolution, I woke up one day wondering where everyone else went. By the early '90's, living deep in the woods along the Canadian border, my head was exploding with acquired knowledge and experiences, but no answers; and certainly little inner peace. In fact the more I ruminated, the less I knew, and a profound burnout set in. Over a prolonged period, I tried to block out the din of head noise and immersed myself in the resolution of personal health problems, a simple backwoods lifestyle and metaphysical contemplation.

I began to experience a fascination with the realization that we live in a three-dimensional realm of consciousness, and that perhaps this was the point of departure that was being overlooked as the point of departure for my understanding. I began to draw triangles and constructs from triangles, and assign values and ideas to the legs and vertices. Being computer illiterate, and I imposed upon my stepson, who was studying computer graphics in college, to translate some of my thoughts into simple drawings. The process was unsatisfactory, so there arose the resolution to return to college to acquire the skills needed to translate inner thoughts into outer expressions. Accordingly I majored in Technical Illustration and Graphic Design, with a Model Building emphasis, and tried to integrate with my studies a personal agenda of learning more about economics and developing writing skills.

At one point in the education process, I wrote a term paper which was an attempt to distill the essence of this three-dimensional obsession (which hopefully will be expanded into a book in the not-to-distant future). For purposes of this discussion, the premise can be stated minimally as follows:

In the three-dimensional plane of consciousness which we inhabit, everything that exists objectively, subjectively or potentially can and must be described in terms of three-dimensional ideas, or Triune Concepts, to be properly understood.

We can picture the mental structure of Triune Concepts as being an equilateral triangle (or a mountain) having a base and an apex. The points at each end of the base represent the opposing poles of a Paradox. The apex represents the unifying point of Oneness, or Transcendence.

Paradox is the apparently self-contradictory polar nature of life.

Transcendence is the abiding point of consciousness which is beyond explanation, yet recognizes truth in Paradox, and represents a quantum step up from dualism to a holistic level of being. It perceives sublime oneness in diversity, divergence and contradiction. It is another name for wisdom.

Demagoguery is the splitting of the Paradox for non-Transcendent or non-analytical purposes.

It is not strictly necessary for the reader of this treatise to consciously absorb this "Triune Concepts" premise to understand the ideas delineated hereinafter. Just understand that the process taken to this degree of conscious definition did represent a unique (as far as I knew then) approach to knowledge, and that it constituted a conceptual architecture upon which the ideas in this book are built. It is the proverbial "method to my madness." It is also, in my view, the key to cutting the Gordian knot on the impasse which currently binds up the "dismal science."

So how is this relevant? The Economics 101 course opened with the assumptions of orthodox economic thought. In the light of my triune mindset, those assumptions and/or the subsequent thought processes appeared to be egregiously flawed. For example, we were taught that economics existed on two levels; i.e., that of "macro-economics" and "micro-economics," each with its own set of rules, parameters and theories. Furthermore, we were told that the distinction between the two should never be confused. Nevertheless, the sequence of thought conveyed through the curriculum commenced to thoroughly muddle the distinction, and that same confusion is compounded in the public discourse.

One way this manifests is that contemporary economic "wisdom" tends to talk about the Federal economy as if it were a "business," with concomitant issues such as "spending," "budgets," and "deficits." We are scolded endlessly about how we must live within our "means," as if those "means" were not the real potential of the tangible economy, but rather the abstract monetary credits pulled out of thin air and assigned artificially to it. The Federal economy is not a business! It is ideally the sovereign macro-economic regime in which businesses operate (notwithstanding the fact that it has effectively become a private business in the portfolio of an extra-national oligarchy due to the abdication by the government of its constitutional responsibility for money creation and regulation to the "Federal Reserve System"). What is more, "spending," "budget" and "deficit" are microeconomic terms, and have no application whatsoever to macroeconomic parameters.

Macro and micro principles and language are commonly lumped together in inappropriate ways, most often by using micro-economic terms for macro-economic concepts. The evident effect is to obfuscate the money creation fraud that is taking place at the macro level.

If one approached the subject with a consciousness that is sufficiently grounded in triune reality, one would immediately recognize that the macro/micro dichotomy represents in actuality the poles of a paradox. It follows from that realization that the terms of the dialogue need to be properly defined, matched and contrasted in juxtaposition to the that fact. From there the whole discussion unfolds quite naturally in a concise and orderly manner that hardly even resembles current normal science or the popular econo-speak. Among other logical conclusions, one eventually awakens to the reality that the so-called "Federal debt" is a contradiction in terms, and a readily dispelled fiscal bogeyman.

This is just a glimpse into the nature of problem. If it seems confusing now, the subject will be expanded in a methodical step-by-step manner further on. Suffice it to say that the fatal defect in the current economic dialogue is not primarily any dullness of mind, paucity of effort, or lack of good faith brought to bear on the issues. The problem is, rather, the largely fallacious assumptions which undergird the discipline, the mis-definition, inadequate lexicon and faulty linking of terms of the dialogue, and the failure to generated sound and meaningful cultural imagery on the subject. All this is compounded by a demagogic thought process that systematically bifurcates economic issues into irreconcilable sides, rather than transcends them in a holistic triune-dimensional vision.

Before proceeding further, some acknowledgements are in order. In an essential sense, the procession of history is woven around the thread of economic history, with a special emphasis on its monetary aspect. This truth is almost totally overlooked in a cultural mythology dominated by the gaudier narrations of wars, rulers and empires. Even histories of social evolution don't quite pick it up. Fortunately, there has been a thin line of scholars, thinkers, churchmen and activists which have kept the dim torch of that knowledge tenuously burning and relayed through the years. It is apropos to acknowledge several who have been instrumental in my awakening. The first is Alexander Del Mar (1836-1926), who is considered by many to be the greatest monetary historian of all time. He was the organizer and director of the US Bureau of statistics, and an actual participant in some of the monetary intrigue of his time. Modern monetary science would be relatively adrift absent his contribution.

Two others are Carl H. Wilken and Charles Walters. Wilken (now deceased), a farmer from Iowa, was regarded as a founder of and the principle advocate for raw materials economics. For a decade, he, along with a handful of close associates, gave more testimony to various Congressional committees than all other non-governmental witnesses combined, and were largely responsible for establishing the principle of structural price parity for raw material and industrial production as the foundation for the economy and the effective backing for the dollar, which in turned was the now unacknowledged factor in pulling the United States out of the Depression, financing WWII, and providing the impetus for post-war recovery. Walters is an economist, journalist, past president of the National Organization for Raw Materials, the founder and editor emeritus for the newspaper Acres USA, the Voice of Eco-Agriculture, and the author of several books. Among other things, he is the chronicler of the legacy of Wilken and associates. His publications of 30 plus years have been a critical doorway into my personal awakening to the subject of economics and monetary science.

Finally I would acknowledge contemporary monetary historian Steven Zarlenga. He and I were for a brief period of time in long-distance contact at the beginning of our respective quests, and exchanged nascent thoughts and research materials. Since then he has gone on to great heights of scholarship, and the authorship of an epic volume which I deem to be the definitive work on the monetary issue for our time. In contrast, my path led through political activism and the distracting vicissitudes of an unsettled personal life. Still, I would aspire to construct some meaningful body of thought upon his scholarly foundation in the by and by.

I have come to realize that we all owe a debt on the monetary question to a long line of public figures from our historical past. This is often quite apart from the virtues, crimes and exploits commonly attributed to them. In fact, it may not be too much to say that their monetary insight and dedication at providential times has made the whole difference in the preservation of this nation. This will be explored in the book as the story unfolds.

I would express appreciation for sources in holy writ, as well as philosophical and metaphysical literature, which have provided orientation, inspiration and manna for the mind and spirit through some trying and formative times. These include, but are not limited to; the Bible, Eastern religious traditions, aboriginal American spirituality, anthropologist Carlos Castaneda, American seer Edgar Cayce, German scholar, philosopher and spiritual scientist Rudolph Steiner, and American transcendentalists Henry David Thoreau and Ralph Waldo Emerson.

Finally, I would acknowledge a debt to every farmer who lovingly tills the soil, every workman who earnestly crafts his vision, every vocalist who passionately sings his song, every artist who captures the elixir of beauty, every child who evokes a smile that lightens the day to gladness, every broken-hearted soul who holds fast to the will to persevere, and every of the countless unheralded others who keep the world turning on its axis. The burden that has been heaped upon the daily lives and dreams of ordinary folk by economic mendacity is of unimaginably crushing magnitude, yet there is an indomitable spirit in humanity that stubbornly refuses to be overcome. A sea of blood cries from the ground on this matter, and it is time that it be met with an answer.

Charles Dickens opened his classic novel *A Tale of Two Cities* with perhaps the most famous of all literary curtain risers (after *"In the beginning,"* that is), i.e. *"It was the best of times, it was the worst of times, ..."* He was referring specifically to the nascent-industrial England of 1775, but the same could have been said more or less of any place or epoch. Indeed, civilization of the modern era has stretched this dichotomy to the uttermost.

We live in a cornucopia of exfoliating progress, possibilities and richness that fairly beggars the imagination. In the last short century or two mankind has plumbed the depths, spanned the heavens, opened the floodgates of material production, developed vast technological capabilities, shrunk the world into a global village, exploded the boundaries of artistic expression, enacted sweeping social and political reforms, unlocked the atom, mastered incredible techniques for healing, and approached the mysteries of the creation of life. Yet, for all of that, it may be fairly asked if we are not approaching the brink of the incomprehensible suicide of civilization, or even the destruction of earth itself, through one or a number of many possible avenues, be it the spontaneous unraveling of the ecosystem, the overwhelming of the last barriers to infectious pandemics, the revitalization of class, ethnic, racial or religious intolerance, the grinding exigencies of agricultural, industrial and service labor, snowballing monetary indebtedness, the ever more maddening pace and dehumanization of modern life, the exhaustion of material resources, the collateral consequences of an imperialist New-World-Order hegemony, nuclear holocaust, or spiritual degeneration.

What are we to think of this impossibly contradictory state of affairs? The meaning, in my view, is that mankind has evolved to the breaking point of the paradoxical nature of existence in this three-dimensional realm of consciousness. The juxtaposed "best" and "worst" of times are in actuality not contradictions, but rather an expression of the poles of the overarching paradox. It has been humankind's wont through the ages to deal dualistically with his dilemmas by dividing them; by pitting one side against the other; by demagoging the issue. The time of reckoning has come where, upon pain of annihilation, that is no longer an option. Our only freedom is to transcend our problems to a wholistic and fully three-dimensional consciousness.

There is a phenomenon in chemistry known as a "super-saturated solution." This is a state in which salt is dissolved in a solution at a concentration which is greater than 100% of what it can theoretically hold, yet it remains dissolved. This occurs because there is no grain of salt in the solution to form a There is a phenomenon in chemistry known as a "super-saturated solution." This is a state in which salt is dissolved in a solution at a concentration which is greater than 100% of what it can theoretically hold, yet it remains dissolved. This occurs because there is no grain of salt in the solution to form a pattern to organize its precipitation. If even the tiniest grain of true form is added in, like magic the excess salt in the solution begins spontaneously to precipitate into a crystal which replicates and amplifies the pattern contained in the initial seed grain.pattern to organize its precipitation. If even the tiniest grain of true form is added in, like magic the excess salt in the solution begins spontaneously to precipitate into a crystal which replicates and amplifies the pattern contained in the initial seed grain.

The state of the macro-political climate at present is analogous. The energy in the hopes, fears, debates, activism, anxieties, heroics, seeking and prayers of the People around the world about the present state of affairs constitutes a mighty socio/economic/political super-saturated immersion. There is a pervasive angst-ridden existential searching out there about having to find a new and better way. Many issues are raised, some which venture tantalizingly close to the next core truth, but we remain yet at a collective loss as to what precisely the problem is, and what exactly can be done about it. If the seed crystal of a true awakening can be sown into the public consciousness, what would precipitate out would be breathtaking. This is no mere metaphor, but a principle of real power and change.

To contribute to the discovery and formulation of that seed grain is the precise purpose of my personal quest. Accordingly, I have established a process, "A New Seed Dialogue," to facilitate the pursuit of that goal. It is an attempt to seek a fresh perspective on the issues of our times by challenging the assumptions, terms and images of the common debate, and establishing an open-ended worldview outside of it. The reader is invited to participate. The nature of the seed grain is triune, and encompasses many areas of inquiry.

It is the hubris of our times that we fancy ourselves modern sophisticates who think "outside the box." This is a culture-wide presumption that intellects of all stripes, hues and abilities are heir to, whether of "conservative," "liberal," "alternative," "hardnosed realistic," "airy-fairy spiritual," or whatever bent. It includes alike the rankest amateur, as well as the most venerated expert. I would argue that in critical ways "the box" has never been more hermetically sealed than it is now. The reason is that we are not sufficiently reckoning with our own enculturation and participation in our civilization's mental stumbling blocks. I say this, not with a critical eye to any particular other person, group or point of view, but as commentary on the besetting state of humanity at present. It behooves all of us (no exceptions), then, to reexamine our own most basic and heartfelt assumptions "to the joint and marrow" in any matter we take on. I daresay the process will be challenging to all persons and persuasions, and it will require heroic intellectual honesty, moral courage and letting go of ego attachment. It will no doubt provoke occasion for much consternation, yet it is the acerbic cup we are obliged to imbibe if we are to persist as a race.

To state the crux of the matter more specifically, we as a people have not come to a realization of the true nature of money; the proliferation of financial sophistication of all stripes notwithstanding. Money is like the wind. It blows through our lives and we feel the buffeting therefrom, but know not whence it comes, nor whither it goes. We put up our sail in whatever niche to catch its currents to power our craft, but it is become an ill wind, and we know not where it is taking us; whether individually, or as a civilization. Human evolution has reached a reckoning where we must at last answer the simple, stark question - "What is Money?"

From the enigmatic wisdom of Don Juan Matus, as related by Carlos Castaneda, comes: *"For me there is only the traveling on paths that have heart, on any path that may have heart. There I travel, and the only worthwhile challenge is to traverse its full length. And there I travel looking, looking breathlessly."* This is a path with heart. You are invited for the journey.

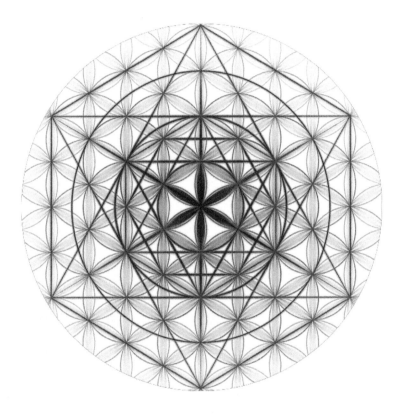

*As in Sacred Geometry, all things fit within the whole to create
a gestalt image greater than the sum of the individual parts.
(This image is for Rich - Elaine)*

Made in the USA
Monee, IL
24 September 2020